Bali

D1386967

- A ☞ in the text denotes a highly recommended sight
- A complete A–Z of practical information starts on p.104
- Extensive mapping on cover flaps

Berlitz Publishing Company, Inc.

Princeton   Mexico City   Dublin   Eschborn   Singapore

22.10.98
THURS
ED. UTSNS
WATERSTONES
EDIN.

Copyright © **1998**, 1995 by Berlitz Publishing Co., Inc.
400 Alexander Park, Princeton, NJ, 08540 USA
9-13 Grosvenor St., London, W1A 3BZ UK

All rights reserved. No part of this book may be reproduced or transmitted in any form or by any means, electronic or mechanical, including photocopying, recording or by any information storage and retrieval system without permission in writing from the publisher.

Berlitz Trademark Reg. U.S. Patent Office and other countries
Marca Registrada

Text:	Martin Gostelow
Editor:	Anne Johnson, Renée Ferguson
Photography:	Pete Bennett
Layout:	Media Content Marketing, Inc.
Cartography:	Visual Image

Found an error we should know about? Our editor would be happy to hear from you, and a postcard would do. Although we make every effort to ensure the accuracy of all the information in this book, changes do occur.

ISBN 2-8315-6288-0
Revised 1997 – First Printing November 1997

Printed in Switzerland by Weber SA, Bienne
019/711 REV

CONTENTS

3

Fact Sheets

Map

BALI and LOMBOK

BALI AND THE BALINESE

Thousands of islands make up the Republic of Indonesia, dividing the Indian Ocean from the Pacific, and Southeast Asia from Australia. Many of them are much bigger than Bali, but they certainly don't come any more famous.

Early visitors brought back tales of a magical culture and happy, beautiful people. Then war and revolution intervened and Bali became an unattainable dream. The next generation of travellers told of a beach-combing idyll, or how they lived with a Balinese family for just a dollar a month. Numbers of visitors grew, and the government and local investors began asking the question: Why give away what we can charge for? The hotel-building boom that started in the 1970s has scarcely eased since, and now people come to Bali in the millions.

Budget accommodation is a cottage industry and prices can be incredibly low, almost reviving the "$5 a day" ambition of 1960s travellers. Others are prepared to spend up to a hundred times as much for seclusion in their own private villa with a view of the ocean or of a valley sculpted into rice terraces a thousand years ago. In between, you can find considerable luxury at a reasonable cost. At all levels, many hotels are built in the form of separate little houses, bungalows, or villas, sometimes found within the walls of a compound. They often imitate traditional Balinese architecture—whether a palace or a rice barn—while in the international resorts architects realize their wildest fantasies,

> Indonesians place emphasis on different ideas of comfort than Westerners do. It may be that the room you consider superior is *less* expensive.

*The beach at Sanur is fringed by coconut palms
and sheltered by a coral reef.*

creating lush, exquisite water gardens, walled villages, gilded pavilions—anything but high-rises, which aren't permitted to spoil the skyline.

Tell someone you are going to Bali and you'll get mixed reactions. It depends on which image they have retained: an untouched paradise; a cultural time-warp; a playground; or somewhere that's just a bit "passé." To the Australians, Bali is the closest exotic getaway, near enough for a long weekend at a lower price than their own tropical north. Surf enthusiasts will know the names of all the tubes and breaks before they arrive, and how to reach the best spots around Bali, Lombok—the next large island to the east of Bali—and the offshore islands. They'll find that many of the young Balinese have overcome their traditional suspicion of the sea as the home of evil spirits and become expert surfers themselves.

From Japan, too, Bali is an easy non-stop flight away and even luxury accommodation looks low-priced when rates are converted to yen. Japanese visitors are younger and more independent these days. At a time when many people are covering up and retreating from the sun, Japanese surfers are out there turning dark brown.

In some countries, growing prosperity leads to a decline in religious belief. This isn't the case in Bali, though, where the majority of people adhere to their version of Hinduism, imported from Java many centuries ago. Villages devote vast sums to expanding and beautifying their temples, and even outside modern concrete shops in the worldliest Kuta street you'll see offerings to the gods: woven palm leaves filled with sweet-scented blossoms, or perfect baskets of rice and other delicious morsels. The gods thus honoured and bad spirits placated—the balance between good and evil must be preserved—Bali's innumerable dogs are free to rifle through the offerings of food. Apparently resigned to their place at the bottom of the pecking order, the poor, mangy creatures are unlikely to starve.

Traditional life goes on behind the doors and walls, and comes out into the open at festival time. Anywhere else in the world, you might hear about the annual festival held in a certain village—naturally at some other time of year; but in Bali, every village has at least three temples, each one has a major festival once a year, and the year is 210 days long. On top of that, every aspect of life is marked by a ceremony, from the sowing of a field to harvest time, or from a baby's first temple visit at one year old, to

Hibiscus flowers are often seen worn over the ear, or used to decorate statues and shrines.

tooth filings (a coming-of-age ritual). Cremations can be so expensive that at times they have to be delayed for years.

Unless you never leave your hotel, you'll be unlucky not to see a colourful celebration of some sort, especially if you take the trouble to ask around. Much of Bali's unique culture is expressed in dance. Little children and lissom teenagers as well as grandmothers are all transformed by classical poses and stylized movements into images of enchanting grace. Performances are staged for the visitors, but that's because the visitors want to see them. Don't fret too much that they are commercial and therefore less genuine—you will at least know when the shows are likely to start! (But be warned, the temple ceremonies are unpredictable: you might be invited for late afternoon and find nothing happening until after midnight.)

By all means take some of the tours. The sites they go to are well worth seeing, in spite of the plague of pushy hawkers

Naming Names

Why do so many Balinese have the same names? Simple. In the vast majority of families, the first-born child is called Wayan, the second Made, the third Nyoman, and the fourth Ketut. At this point the list, short as it is, runs out and starts again from the beginning. Thus the fifth child is another Wayan, the sixth another Made, and so on. So when you meet a Ketut, he or she could be the fourth or eighth child in a family—or the twelfth, but that is a rarity these days.

Among the Ksatria caste, descended from the old ruling families, first-born boys and girls can be given the names Gede or Putu (and other castes sometimes copy this fashion).

Traditionally there were no surnames, and even now very few people have them. To tell the difference between all the Wayans and Mades, they may have a second name, perhaps referring to the way they looked or behaved as children.

and ranks of souvenir shops outside their entrances. You will have to get used to paying a host of fees and donations: temples and even whole villages have donation books where you write in your name and contribution. There is no need to match the sums apparently contributed by previous visitors. A lot of local people realise that the commercialism can be a deterrent ("No hassle!" some signs promise), and a few temples regulate the hawkers and keep stalls at a distance. Even in the crowded south, the ugliness is restricted to the main roads—so get off them and walk along the footpaths

Temples can be the best places to enjoy the arts of Bali, from dance to intricate wood carving.

among the rice paddies, where you will find the duck shepherds taking their flocks to feed and splash.

Bali is a shopper's heaven if you are looking for bargain beachwear and casual clothes, souvenirs, or craftwork. Most of the crafts have been adapted to the tourist and export trades and are now produced in vast quantities. Ancient skills have been applied to new subjects without drastically debasing standards, and something quite fresh and inventive seems to appear each year. The workers are truly versatile, turning to new materials, designs, and techniques unknown to their parents' generation. The painted tropical fish and birds, for example, weren't made at all until 20 years ago; and the quilted bedcovers are newer still. A lot of the proceeds of this booming trade are spent by the successful villages in staging extravagant and flamboyant ceremonies and beautifying their temples.

Not all of Bali's industry is a matter of wood carving and hand weaving—the chances are that the rugged Jeep-type vehicle you rent for a drive round the island was assembled in a factory near Denpasar. The height of ambition for the young Balinese is to buy a motorcycle, not least because it's seen as essential for courtship—or a discreet affair—but also for employment outside their villages. You will notice that hotel staff car parks are a sea of motorbikes and scooters, and that's how the dancers in the evening performance will most likely arrive, too, looking a little different, dressed in T-shirts and jeans.

Ownership of a motorbike seems to act as an incentive to keep families small: a father, mother, and their two children

A character in the Ramayana Ballet portrays the garuda bird, long identified with Bali.

can just about ride together, but more could be a problem. Despite this, there is no shortage of children yet, with neatly uniformed tribes of scholars trooping or cycling to school in shifts starting at 6:30 A.M., and coming home again at all hours from 11:30 A.M. to 2:00 P.M.

Everywhere you go you'll hear cries of "Hello, hello! *Dari mana?* (Where are you from?)" "Too many tourists!" some visitors grumble, while never leaving the tourist resorts. It's no good lamenting that Bali has become a holiday magnet. Take it for what it is. You'll discover that any of its advantages still far outweigh the faults. Of all the tropical destinations where warm seas and sunshine attract holiday-makers from all corners of the world, this one has a resilient and unique culture, as well as remarkable, adaptable people.

Facts & Figures

Area
Indonesia: 1,905,000 square km (735,000s quare miles)
Bali: 5,623 square km (2,171 square miles)
Lombok: 4,738 square km (1,829 square miles)

Population
Indonesia: 195,000,000
Bali: 3,000,000
Lombok: 2,500,000

Religion
Indonesia: 95% Muslim
Bali: 95% Bali-Hindu, others Muslim, Christian, Buddhist
Lombok: 75% Muslim, others Wektu Telu, Bali-Hindu

Climate
Tropical, hot and humid
Wet season: December–March
Dry season: June–September
Intermediate months are changeable

A BRIEF HISTORY

The famous fossil remains of the "Java Man" show that the species *Homo erectus*, a predecessor of the modern human race, lived in Java between two million and 500,000 years ago. Much later, around 10,000 B.C., the evidence points to the presence of a Neolithic culture in Bali and Java. But today's Indonesians mainly descend from migrants who came from south China via the Malay peninsula and moved along the island chain to Bali, Lombok, and beyond, from 3000 to 1000 B.C. Archaeological finds show that there was a flourishing Bronze Age culture in Bali and Lombok between about 1000 and 100 B.C. A bronze drum, dating back to around 300 B.C., found in Bali (see page 47) resembles those made in what is today northern Vietnam, but whether it's an import or a local copy is not known. Trade and cultural exchanges with Southeast Asia had certainly begun by then, and there were frequent contacts with India by A.D. 100. About this time, too, wet rice cultivation was introduced to Bali, changing the face of the countryside to that of its present appearance of rice paddy fields and terraces.

> Indonesian and Malay (spoken in Malaysia) are almost the same languages. The principal difference is in the spelling.

Indian traders and teachers brought Buddhism to Java. It had only a limited influence in Bali, however, where people continued in their ancient animist beliefs, worshipping the spirits of the mountains, rivers, and other natural forces.

Hinduism Comes to Bali

In the 8th and 9th centuries A.D., several Buddhist rulers in Java converted to Hinduism, along with their subjects. This

Historical Landmarks

3000-1000 B.C. Migration from southern China via Malay peninsula and along the island chain of Indonesia.

ca. 1000-100 B.C. Bronze Age culture in Bali and Lombok.

ca. A.D. 100 Trade and cultural exchanges with Southeast Asia and India. Beginning of wet rice cultivation.

8th-9th centuries Hindu kingdoms replace Buddhist kingdoms in Java; Hinduism spreads to Bali.

10th-13th centuries Bali independent at times or ruled by Java.

1294 Majapahit empire founded in Java.

1343 Majapahit Gajah Mada reconquers Bali.

1400-1500 Rise of Islam in Java.

ca. 1500 Java's Hindu rulers, priests, and scholars flee to Bali.

1550 Bali and Lombok ruled by Dewa Agung (god-king) of Gelgel.

1597 Dutch expedition under de Houtman arrives off Bali.

17th-18th centuries Isolation. Bali splits into ten rajadoms.

1846-49 Dutch military expeditions.

1850-1900 The Dutch establish control over most of Bali.

1906 Dutch force marches on Denpasar. The Raja of Badung and his court commit mass suicide.

1920s-30s Foreign artists bring Balinese culture to world notice.

1927 Sukarno and others form nationalist party, PNI.

1942 Japanese occupy Indonesia, exploiting its oil and rice.

1945 World War II ends. Sukarno and Hatta proclaim republic.

1946-49 Dutch attempt to re-establish control over Indonesia.

1950 (17 August) Republic of Indonesia recognized by Dutch.

1963 Eruption of Gunung Agung devastates Bali.

1965 Six generals murdered in failed coup; communists blamed.

1965-66 Widespread revenge killings of communists and others.

1968 Suharto becomes president.

1980s Rapid increase of tourism. Many luxury resorts are built.

time, many people in Bali followed suit, perhaps attracted by the complex Hindu mythology—the Balinese today still have a love of the old stories—and by the way, their local gods could easily be housed in the crowded Hindu pantheon. Around 930, the kingdom of East Java conquered Bali and the conversion process accelerated. A mild form of the caste system and the concept of the Hindu trinity of Brahma, Shiva, and Vishnu were introduced. But Bali was no mere vassal state of Java. From 1019 to 1042, Airlangga, son of the Balinese king Udayana and a Javanese princess, ruled over East Java, while his young brother acted as regent in Bali. During the 12th and 13th centuries, Bali was often independent.

A powerful Hindu empire named after its capital, Majapahit, united all of Java by 1320. The Majapahit general Gajah Mada reconquered Bali in 1343, and added a large part of the Indonesian archipelago besides. Hindu art and scholarship spread through the islands, but in most of them their flowering was to be rather short-lived. With the death in 1389 of King Hayam Wurukin, its last great ruler, the empire of Majapahit began to decline.

Muslim traders and teachers had already started converting several of Java's princes and people to Islam, especially in coastal areas, and in the 14th and 15th centuries the movement gathered pace and spread to the interior. By around the year 1500, seeing their world breaking up, many Majapahit aristo-

Built up over two thousand years, Bali's rice terraces are a hallmark of the landscape.

crats, priests, and scholars fled to Bali, where their culture continued to flourish. Islam never gained a strong foothold in Bali, which had few products to attract traders and, because of its many reefs and lack of harbours, was difficult to invade. The early 16th century also brought the first European ships to Indonesian waters, when the Portuguese came in search of spices and set up trading posts—though not on Bali.

In 1550 Bali was united under Batu Renggong, the formidable ruler known as Dewa Agung (god-king) of Gelgel, near Klungkung. His men even succeeded in turning back the tide of Islam for a short while, adding eastern Java and Lombok to his domains. During his rule, Balinese power, culture, and influence reached a peak, with a boom in temple building and the associated crafts of sculpture and woodcarving.

The future colonial power, the Dutch, appeared briefly on the scene in 1597 when the battered remnants of an expedition

The market at Sweta, Lombok. Red chilli peppers are a feature of the local cooking.

under de Houtman anchored off the coast of Bali.

When he decided to sail away and return to the Netherlands, three of his men stayed behind to serve the Dewa Agung. Almost 250 years passed before the Dutch tried to exert any real control here, in sharp contrast to Java, which they ruthlessly exploited. Left to their own devices, Bali's rulers fell to squabbling among themselves and the island split into ten or more rajadoms. A 17th-century Dewa Agung moved the royal capital from Gelgel to nearby Klungkung, but the balance of power shifted from one rajadom to another, notably Bululeng in the north and then Karangasem in the east (which also seized most of Lombok). Bali's contact with the Dutch was restricted to providing slaves—mainly Balinese who had broken the rajas' laws or priests' taboos—and soldiers for the army of the United Dutch East Indies Company (*Vereenigde Oostindische Compagnie,* or VOC). The company was the instrument of influence of the Netherlands until it went bankrupt in 1799 and was superseded by the government.

Between 1811 and 1817, during the Napoleonic Wars, Britain took control of Indonesia and seriously thought of staying once the wars were over. Britain's administrator, Stamford Raffles, who was named Lieutenant Governor, even visited Bali, and may have had it in mind to build a trading station here. After the war, however, the British government decided to restore Dutch territory and interests—and Raffles found another site, the island and future port of Singapore.

The Dutch Take Over

Once re-established in Java, the Dutch tried to foster trade with Bali, aiming to increase their influence and also to prevent the Balinese from plundering ships wrecked off the coast. They failed, and their frustration was perpetuated by the fact that a Danish trader called Mads Lange was enjoying great success in Bali. Following the looting of a ship in 1841, the Dutch negotiated a treaty with Bali's rajas which they thought guaranteed an end to such practices. When it became clear that the Balinese didn't see it that way at all, the Dutch then decided for the first time to use force. Some 1,600 men, recruited mainly in the Moluccas and other Indonesian islands, landed on the north coast in 1846 and burned Singaraja. The Balinese prepared for a battle, but before it could take place, Mads Lange persuaded the two sides to sign a truce. The rajas agreed to stop the plundering of wrecks, and to pay compensation for the 1841 incident, but it soon emerged that they had no intention of sticking to the deal, and in 1848 the Dutch landed their second military expedition in the north of Bali. Advancing inland to attack the Balinese base at Jagaraga, they were ambushed by a bigger but less well-armed force led by Jelantik, younger brother of the Raja of Bululeng. In spite of appalling losses, the Balinese won the day. The defeated Dutch invaders retreated in disorder to their ships.

Such a humiliation could not go unavenged, and the following year, a third Dutch military expedition, far stronger than its predecessors, landed near Singaraja. The northern rajadoms sued for peace; they were offered terms calling for them to disarm and submit to Dutch rule. The response of Jelantik was to fall back to Jagaraga and prepare to fight. This time the Balinese were overwhelmed and thousands were killed, some in a suicidal march towards enemy guns, a ritual death in battle known as *puputan*. After a second Dutch landing at Padangbai Bay, the *puputan* ritual was repeated when the Raja of Karangasem and his family threw themselves on the enemy guns.

For the rest of the 19th century, the Dutch, using the rajas and other aristocrats as regents, took control over most of Bali, but their influence in the south remained limited. This was emphasized in 1904 when a ship wrecked off Sanur was plundered of its cargo. The Dutch demanded reparations for this act; the southern rajas refused. In 1906 a force of mainly Moluccan troops led by Dutch officers marched on Denpasar to enforce compliance. They found the place almost deserted, until suddenly the Raja of Badung, together with his family and hundreds of courtiers, emerged from the palace. On a

Pura Penataran Sasih — site of a Bronze-Age drum that some say fell from the sky.

signal from the raja, one of his priests stabbed him with a *kris* (knife), and then, pausing only to stab their children first, the rest of the royal party began a *puputan*, either killing themselves or running suicidally towards the enemy. When the dreadful scene was repeated by the Dewa Agung and his wives and followers in 1908 in front of the palace at Klungkung, the rajas' resistance to Dutch rule was at an end.

The public in the Netherlands were appalled by these grisly events. From then on, Bali and the Balinese came to be looked on as unique, to be protected from the colonial treatment that had turned the other islands into plantations exploited for profit. Tourism was discouraged, although a few foreigners did make the journey and brought back with them news of the island's extraordinary culture to the outside world. Some artists came in the 1920s and a few stayed, both influencing Balinese painting styles and being influenced by them.

In the way of most colonial powers, the Netherlands began the considerate processes that were to lead to its own demise. Many young Indonesians received a Dutch education, with the brightest students going to universities in the Netherlands. The Dutch language gave the vast polyglot archipelago a sense of unity, even among islands that had been bitter enemies for centuries. Between 1910 and 1930, Indonesians began to form a variety of radical political groups, namely nationalist, religious, socialist, and also communist. Strikes were organized and minor insurrections erupted. Then in 1927 a graduate engineer, Sukarno, along with others, formed a nationalist association which was to evolve into the Partai Nasional Indonesia, or PNI. Sukarno was imprisoned for four years in 1929 as a political agitator. On release, he soon resumed his activities, only to be arrested again and sent into internal exile, first on Flores and later on the island of Sumatra.

War and Independence

Early in 1942, soon after their attacks on Pearl Harbor and Singapore, the Japanese invaded and occupied Indonesia, with the intention of exploiting its oil and rice. It suited them to work with the Indonesian nationalists led by Mohammad Hatta and Sukarno, who hoped to extract concessions in return. Indonesians replaced the Dutch administrators, who had either fled or been interned.

In the dying days of World War II, the Japanese promised to hand over power to Indonesia's nationalist leaders. In the event, it happened that the decision was not theirs to make. Following the Japanese surrender on 14 August 1945, Sukarno and Hatta proclaimed Indonesia an independent republic on 17 August, with Sukarno as its first president.

The years 1946 to 1949 saw the Dutch trying to reassert control. Recovering from years of Nazi occupation, they could not muster the huge forces needed to take all the islands, but they were able to seize major cities and the eastern islands, and to launch so-called "police actions" against the nationalist-held areas, primarily in Java.

In Bali, a young colonel in the nationalist army, Ngurah Rai, organized a force to resist the return of the Dutch, but it was not strong enough to oppose their landing early in 1946. The nationalists retreated into the hills to conduct a guerrilla campaign, and in November 1946 they found themselves trapped close to Marga, north of Tabenan. Outnumbered and outgunned, Ngurah Rai and all 96 of his followers were killed in what is regarded as the last *puputan*. Their sacrifice is commemorated by a monument and museum at the site, together with stones bearing the names of each of those who died on the island of Bali during the struggle for independence (see page 68).

Eventually, under pressure from the U.N. and the United States, which used post-war aid as a lever, the Dutch were forced to give up the attempt to rebuild their colonial empire. On 17 August 1950, five years to the day after independence was first declared, the fledgling Republic of Indonesia was recognized by the Netherlands.

The 1955 Afro-Asian conference in Bandung heralded the arrival of the new nation, and its leader Sukarno was welcomed to the world stage. Together with India's Nehru and Tito of Yugoslavia, he was credited with the foundation of the non-aligned movement.

The mythical garuda bird is a national symbol and a standard subject for Bali's woodcarvers.

Years of Confusion

A succession of short-lived coalition governments wrestled with the problems posed by separatist movements on the various island groups, dislocation caused by war and its aftermath, a badly neglected infrastructure, and the colonial legacy of over-exploited plantations. Frustrated by Indonesia's loss of direction, Sukarno declared a form of martial law in 1957. A so-called "guided democracy" and an appointed national council and non-party government took the place of the elected assembly and ineffectual coalitions.

The period between 1959 and 1965 was a surreal time of government by means of slogans and Orwellian acronyms. Sukarno attempted to control the competing nationalist, religious, and communist groups; NASAKOM was the word he used to represent their supposed common interests. As if that wasn't enough, processions paraded with placards emblazoned with MANIPOL (Sukarno's political manifesto) and DEKON (his economic declaration) written on them, and there were others which condemned NEKOLIM (neo-colonialism and imperialism). In the meantime, the Indonesian economy collapsed and hyper-inflation destroyed the currency.

The country's limited foreign-exchange reserves were squandered on prestigious projects, grand monuments, and stadia to host the Asian Games of 1962, seen as a showpiece for the nation. Travel agents were given a tour, including a visit to Bali that coincided with an important ceremony in March 1963 at the so-called "mother temple" Besakih, on the slopes of the island's highest mountain, Gunung Agung. A long dormant volcano, it chose this particular moment to begin emitting smoke and firing rocks into the air, but the ceremony went ahead anyway, literally under a cloud. The official guests had scarcely left Bali when Gunung Agung exploded in what was the most violent eruption the island

Mt. Batur, rising above Penelokan, is one of Bali's many active volcanoes.

had seen in centuries. Lava flowed down its slopes, but despite the impressions conveyed by the stories still told now (and the photographs seen in many books), it covered only a limited area. The chief instrument of destruction was the volcanic ash that showered down on the northern half of Bali, covering it with a layer typically 40 centimeters (15 inches) thick. Crops were wiped out; the rice terraces were devastated, and starvation threatened.

A more immediate disaster added to the islanders' woes. The ash had blocked rivers, and the dams it formed could not retain the waters for long. When they broke, torrents of mud and rock tore down the valleys and through the villages and towns along the river banks. The official death toll of 1,600 was certainly a wild underestimate. The sky had been black even over southern Bali, although the capital Denpasar received only a sprinkling of ash.

Coup and Revenge

On 30 September 1965, a group of army conspirators based near Indonesia's capital, Jakarta, kidnapped and killed six army generals. The circumstances have never been fully explained, although the murderers claimed they acted to prevent a possible coup against Sukarno. In the following days, General Suharto, one of the most senior surviving commanders, moved speedily to isolate the conspirators and effectively seized power. The blame for the killings was pinned on the Communist Party, the PKI, who denied any involvement. A pogrom was then unleashed, first in Java and next in Bali, with widespread killings of communists, in revenge and also to settle old scores. The Chinese minority, mainly shopkeepers, moneylenders, and other small businesspeople, were another target. In common with the other immigrant groups, they had been compelled by law to display the flag of their country of origin, even if a century had passed since their ancestors had left it. So every Chinese business was marked by the flag of China—communist China—and associated in people's minds with communism. The numbers killed will never be known: in Bali alone the total casualties may have exceeded 60,000.

Banks do not like changing worn *foreign* notes.

Sukarno's association with the PKI and suspicion of his involvement in the coup cost him much of his popularity and authority. Only his honoured role in the independence struggle saved him from trial. The army forced him to yield most of his powers to Suharto, who in 1968 took over the presidency itself. Sukarno died two years later.

Growth and Modernization

In the decades following, the economy stabilized as growing oil revenues fuelled expansion. The Chinese community carefully rebuilt its commercial interests, this time much less visibly. Tourism to Bali was seen as a money-spinner: the 1970s saw a rapid increase in the numbers of foreign visitors. During the 1980s, the authorities' strategy was to develop more profitable business; and they designated Nusa Dua as a huge tourist enclave where only luxury hotels would be built. To bring the necessary volume of visitor traffic to fill all the new rooms, Denpasar Airport's runway was extended out into the sea to handle big airliners.

The holiday market is hungry for new places and the government is eager to create jobs and earn foreign currency. These are the two factors that transformed Bali, and they have slowly begun to take effect in next-door Lombok, too. You may be here to relax and enjoy a slower pace, but there's no escaping the fact that Indonesia is an important part of the world's fastest-growing economic region.

WHERE TO GO

Don't expect—and don't even try—to rush around seeing all the temples and other cultural attractions on the island, or all those mentioned in this section. The island scenery and catching glimpses of everyday life are just as rewarding. Best of all is to turn a corner and find a procession, perhaps the whole population of a village, dressed in their best and blocking the road. Mere buildings, however beautifully they are carved, can seem quite sterile when nothing is going on. We have selected some of the most interesting and important attractions, but to truly appreciate and absorb what you see, we suggest that you take a few at a time.

Start as soon after dawn as possible, when it's cool; also, the light is better for photography, the roads are quieter, and the sites themselves are not as crowded. Even the ubiquitous vendors who station themselves strategically near all the well-known places and usually won't take no for an answer seem less pushy early in the day. A prompt start also gives you extra time to reach the more remote areas. You can get to any part of Bali in a day, but you will cut travelling times and add interest if you make overnight stays in different parts of the island.

THE SOUTHERN RESORTS

Most of Bali's tourism is concentrated into a tiny fraction of the island, with the vast majority of visitors heading for the "big three" beaches, namely **Sanur, Kuta,** and **Nusa Dua**, all within a short drive of the airport. Some stretches of sand are so magnificent and the water so warm, it's hard to believe that they were ignored for so long by the Balinese people, who have traditionally turned away from the sea. Now visitors come in the millions from all over the world with little in mind but sun, sand, warm seas, and watersports.

Sanur

Southeast of Denpasar, Bali's capital, is where the first modern hotel was built next to any of Bali's beaches, 10 storeys high, in the 1960s. Fortunately, the authorities decreed that in the future no building should be higher than a palm tree. The tower was gutted by fire in 1993, except Room 327, which was hardly damaged and has been preserved in its smoke-blackened state as a shrine to the fact that everyone in the hotel escaped unharmed. The rest of the building was restored, completely modernized, and reopened as the Grand Bali Beach Hotel.

The rest of Sanur has been sprucing itself up, too, to avoid being left behind by the newer resorts. In atmosphere, it falls somewhere between the brash, noisy Kuta and secluded Nusa Dua. Mostly half-hidden by trees, many of Sanur's hotels face the beach. It's an adequate stretch of sand, if not the island's best, and only good for swimming at high tide.

Just inland, parallel to the coast, the village looks at first like nothing more than a long strip of souvenir shops, clothing boutiques, and restaurants. But take a walk along some of the lanes leading off the main road, Jalan Tanjung Sari, or beyond the impatient traffic of the bypass (Jalan Bypass) and you'll find traditional life still going on as if tourism had never happened.

Only a short walk north along the shore from the Grand Bali Beach Hotel is the **Le Mayeur Museum,** once the house of the Belgian painter. He came to Bali in 1932 and stayed to marry the beautiful Ni Pollok, who had been a well-known *legong* dancer (see page 86) before retiring (at 14!) to teach dance. In its day, the garden with its ponds and statues was open on the seaward side; now it is fully enclosed. The outside of the house is covered with stone carvings while the interior is a gallery of sculpture collected by Le Mayeur. The walls are hung with his own paintings: European landscapes, Balinese scenes, and studies of dancers, including Ni Pollok. When Le Mayeur died in 1958, the house was turned into a museum that his widow ran until her death in 1985.

Local fishermen ponder their chances of a possible catch near the resort enclave of Nusa Dua.

Near the small harbour at this end of Sanur Beach you can find a motorized *prahu* (outrigger boat) to take you to **Nusa Lembongan**, an island 17 km (11 miles) offshore to the east, which is noted for its good surfing and snorkelling.

Along at the southern end of Sanur Beach, near the Sanur Beach Hotel, the signs point to **Pura Belanjong**. It's only a short walk, but few people find their way to this old temple, deserted

---

Old Hands

Kuta's beach masseuses are an institution: some have been operating here for 20 years. In the heat of the day they understandably prefer to work in the shade of an awning. Negotiate a price first and check that there's no sand on you, on the cloth where you'll be lying, or on the masseuse's hands. Otherwise you'll feel as if you've been rubbed with sandpaper. Massage has a central and respected role in Balinese healing, and although the beach version is rudimentary, some of the hotels employ skilled practitioners like those in Sweden.

Highlights

The Southern Resorts and Denpasar (pages 27-40)
Bukit Peninsula: Uluwatu temple; Suluban surfing beach.
Denpasar: Museum Negeri Propinsi Bali; Arts Centre.

From Denpasar to Ubud (pages 40-50)
Ubud: Museum Puri Lukisan; Museum Neka.
Petulu: herons glide in to nest at sundown.
Goa Gajah "Elephant Cave": below the road east of Teges.
Yeh Pulu rock sculptures: dating back to 14th century.
Tampaksiring: Gunung Kawi shrines, Tirta Empul temple spring.

Eastern Bali (pages 50-56)
Klungkung: Kerta Gosa, Royal Hall of Justice, ceiling.
Tenganan Bali Aga: original Balinese village.
Tirtagangga: water gardens and rice fields.

The Mountains (pages 56-62)
Bangli: Pura Kehen, chief temple of Bangli's former rajadom.
Batur: views of caldera, Mount Batur, and Lake Batur.
Besakih: Bali's mother temple and complex of temples.
Bedugul and Lake Beratan: hill resort near lakes and volcanoes.

The North Coast (pages 62-67)
Sangsit: Pura Beji — most elaborate temple in the north.
Jagaraga: temple known for its strange carved stone decorations.
Kambutambahan: Pura Maduwe Karang — famous carving.

West of Denpasar (pages 67-71)
Mengwi: Pura Taman Ayun, temple noted for its double moat.
Sangeh Monkey Forest: grove of protected nutmeg trees.
Tanah Lot: most photographed sea temple in Bali.
Negara: decorated water buffaloes race against each other.

Lombok (pages 71-81)
Cakranegara: Pura Meru, Mayura Water Palace.
Suranadi: Temple of the Holy Eels and gardens.
Senggigi: beaches and coastal scenery to the north.
The Gilis: diving and snorkelling and relative solitude.
Gunung Rinjani: mountain treks, crater, lake, and craft villages.

unless there's a ceremony. A stone pillar, now set in a pit and protected by railings, bears an inscription said to date from A.D. 913, but as it is normally wrapped in cloth you're unlikely to see it.

When the tide is at its lowest, you can pick your way out to the offshore reef—remember to wear shoes for protection against the sharp coral and spiny sea urchins. If you time it right, it's possible to wade out to Nusa Serangan, or Turtle Island, from the beach south of Belanjong. The only problem is that when the tide starts to come in, you'll soon find yourself marooned and boatmen can charge you an extortionate amount to take you back (and you have to wait until there's enough water to get across). The island, a low sandspit with a couple of villages and some sad captive turtles, is hardly worth it.

Kuta

The most famous stretch of beach in Bali forms the western shore of a narrow neck of land just north of the airport. After young travellers discovered in the late 1960s that they could enjoy a back-to-nature existence here at minimal cost, they gathered in ever-increasing numbers. Tales were told in Australia about the "perfect wave," and Kuta became the dream destination for every surfer. Once a poor fishing village, it was transformed into a frenetic scene, fuelled by plenty of alcohol and, for a while, illegal drugs. The height limit was virtually the only regulation applied to building, and a scruffy shanty town soon sprang up. Never previously a problem in Bali, theft and prostitution (chiefly blamed on incomers from the other islands) looked as if they were becoming endemic. On and off the beach, every foreigner was plagued by hawkers as adhesive as bush flies.

Eventually, voices were heard at *banjar* meetings urging a clean-up and the raising of standards. Today Kuta has cleaned itself up and gone a long way towards putting its house right.

Bali is a study in contrasts, offering scores of shrines like this one, and picture-perfect beaches.

Drugs have largely disappeared and crime rates are down, although you still need to beware of pickpockets and shouldn't leave property unguarded. The quality of hotels and homestays, old and new, has improved, with price increases to match. In keeping with its new image Kuta has begun to acquire the trappings of a modern town, in the form of the multi-storey Kuta Centre and Galleria shopping and leisure complexes.

The big unsolved problem is traffic—in spite of the one-way system, the roads are more congested than ever with surfers on motorbikes carrying their boards, hundreds of kids cycling to school, *bemos*, and tourists in Jeeps. Moneychangers, clothes shops, car and bike rental agencies, all sorts of accommodation, and numerous bars and restaurants line every street and *gang* (alley).

The beach is the reason to be here, and even though you won't escape the hawkers, it's a rest cure after the bustle of the town. The tide washes most of the sand twice a day and beachfront hotels clean up their local areas. Swim only between the flags, where Australian-style lifeguards keep watch: the undertow and currents can be hazardous.

Towards sunset, a golden light reflects off the sea and local people come out to stroll or paddle in the shallows. Young men play soccer on the sand or join the tourists in a volleyball game, while the eager beach masseuses rustle up a new wave of business.

At nightfall, new choices beckon. You can inspect Bali's selection of shops, pick a restaurant, go on a pub crawl, or see a movie and wait for midnight when the discos get into gear.

Kuta's Neighbours

Kuta Beach can mean the small area around the original village, or the whole coast stretching from the airport north to Legian and beyond. When the down-market reputation of Kuta a few years ago deterred travel companies, its neighbours set out to establish a separate identity. **Tuban Beach** to the south has half a dozen big hotels and a waterpark with waterslides and a swimming pool, attracting families and groups. The beach and streets are quieter, the shops a bit less brash, and the big restaurants mainly bright and modern.

Adjoining Kuta to the north, **Legian** at first seems like more of the same, with a big concentration of places to eat, drink, dance, and sleep along Jalan Melasti, Jalan Padma, and Jalan Legian itself. Sunrise is an idyllic time to be on Legian Beach. Surfers are out at the first light of dawn and runners pace the water's edge. The farther north you go, the less congested the streets and the beach, until you can almost find yourself standing alone on the broad sands of **Seminyak**.

North again, surfers find their way to **Canggu Beach** by way of narrow tracks through the rice fields. The final kilometre or so is passable only by motorbike or on foot.

Bukit Badung

Referred to simply as Bukit (or "the hill") by the Balinese, the peninsula south of the airport is almost a separate island. Most of it is a windswept limestone plateau, entirely unlike the rest of southern Bali. Too dry for rice, its rocky soil is

The Chinese temple at Benoa.

used to grow beans, cassava, and peanuts. In the past, few people lived here, and the only reason they might visit was to worship at one of the temples and particularly at Uluwatu on the cliffs at the western tip. Then came the 1980s and the demand for more upscale and luxury hotels. To spread the load and pressure away from Kuta and Sanur, the government picked the east side of the Bukit peninsula as the site to develop a new resort.

At **Nusa Dua**, the outside world—even the everyday Balinese world—is excluded. There's little traffic or noise, and no hassle from hawkers in this neatly manicured park. A dozen luxury hotels are half-hidden among the palm trees next to the dazzling white beach, with two championship golf courses, a convention centre, and a modern shopping and restaurant complex in the same area. The name, meaning "two islands," refers to two knobs of land sticking out from the coast in the middle of the reserve. They are not true islands but are each connected by a narrow neck of land. Predictably, a ramshackle village has grown up just outside the resort, with the souvenir shops and many of the restaurants undercutting the hotels.

Lower-priced hotels and more eating places line the 5 km (3 miles) of coast north of Nusa Dua all the way to **Benoa**. Once a dusty, somnolent fishing village, this has turned into a water-sports centre of buzzing jet skis, motorboats, diving centres, and bars.

Don't confuse Benoa village with **Benoa Port**, on the opposite (north) side of the muddy inlet known as Benoa Harbour. Reached from the Sanur-Kuta road by a long causeway, this is where cargo ships tie up. There is a charge for driving along the causeway to the jetty, and no reason for going to the end unless you plan to take the fast twin-hull ferry to Lombok, a cruise to Nusa Lembongan, or a deep-sea fishing trip.

Jimbaran Beach is a great arc of sand facing a sheltered bay south of the airport, shared by a handful of resort hotels and a fishing village. More hotels are rapidly going up on a new access road that runs parallel to the coast here. Look for the sign to Uluwatu off the road from the airport towards Nusa Dua—you have to go past it and make a U-turn.

The road across the Bukit peninsula climbs past limestone quarries to a height of 200 meters (660 feet) on its way to the western tip of land and **Pura Luhur Uluwatu**. All the way up the long flight of steps of this temple, and especially near the shrines, you'll be eyed by fairly friendly monkeys. If they have

Water lilies add to the tropical floral splendour of Bali with their striking colour.

already been well fed by visitors ahead of you, they won't bother troubling you—but hide your possessions in advance just in case they're hungry. Bus tours converge on Uluwatu towards sunset, so if you want the place to yourself and you don't mind missing the standard photo opportunity, go at another time.

Just to the north of the parking area for Uluwatu, a sign points to **Suluban Beach**, 2 km (1½ miles) down a narrow, rough track. Motorcycles can make it most of the way and young locals sometimes wait around to ferry those who need a ride. Everyone has to walk the last part to the cliff top, where cement steps lead down to the shore.

DENPASAR

The capital of Bali since the end of World War II, Denpasar was still a small market town only 20 years ago. Now ten times the size, fuelled by prosperity from the tourism boom, with all the government institutions and buildings to match its status, it's a noisy, polluted urban sprawl. Rush hour lasts most of the day, and when traffic lights change there's a cavalry charge of motorcycles and scooters. In the middle of it all, the better-off live in traditional family compounds—extra-high walls are the main concession to this kind of life. Those who have had to adapt to apartment living in the city can still have their family temple—on the roof!

The most prominent central landmark is a big grey statue of the four-faced Hindu god Catur Muka, looking each way at the main intersection. The one-way system here sends traffic north up **Jalan Veteran** (Veteran Street) or east along **Jalan Surapati,** which, after changes of name, becomes the road to Sanur. West of the intersection, **Jalan Gaja Mada** is lined by banks, shops, and restaurants. It soon meets Jalan Sulawesi and then the dirty and usually rather smelly Badung River. The city's main fresh produce market, **Pasar**

Badung, jams a four-storey building and is open from before dawn until midday. Just across the river is a similar building housing the handicraft and textile market, Pasar Kumbasari.

The colonial **Bali Hotel** stands on both sides of Jalan Veteran. A little farther along on the left there's another market, flowing out into the adjoining street. About 1 km (1/2 mile) along Jalan Veteran, the **bird market** caters to the local liking for caged birds, from big hornbills to tiny songsters.

The big area of grass south of Jalan Surapati is **Alun-alun Puputan** (Puputan Square), site of the *puputan* or mass suicide in 1906 of the Raja of Badung's court (see page 20).

Pura Luhur Uluwatu at the tip of Bukit Peninsula.

Bali Museum (Museum Negeri Propinsi Bali)

At the farthest corner of Puputan Square, its red brick and grey stone buildings inside a walled compound echo the traditional Balinese palace and temple architecture. Dating from the colonial era of the early 20th century, some of the displays look as if they may not have been changed since then, apart from the removal of Dutch labels. There are good

Which Beach?

Here are the main options, with their plus and minus points.

Sanur: long-established beach hotels; shops and restaurants; sand beach but rocks restrict swimming at low tide. Atmosphere is somewhere between noisy Kuta and peaceful Nusa Dua. (See pages 28-31)

Kuta: a huge sandy beach; good surfing, but swimming requires caution; the biggest choice of accommodation; plenty of clothes shops; a mainly young crowd and the most active night scene on Bali. (See pages 31-33)

Legian: vast beach; surfing and swimming with care; plenty of bars, discos, and restaurants at southern end where it adjoins Kuta; the north end is relatively tranquil. (See page 33)

Tuban Beach: the quieter continuation of Kuta beach southward; mostly larger hotels; a less hectic street scene but plenty of restaurants; family-oriented. (See page 33)

Nusa Dua: a resort enclave with a fine sandy beach; sailing and safe swimming; some hotels are far from outside shops and restaurants; isolated from island life and sights. (See page 34)

Jimbaran Beach: just a few hotels; superb gently shelving beach; sailing and safe swimming; a small village nearby; south of the airport and some way from most tourist sights. (See page 35)

Candi Dasa: narrow beach of grey sand and stones, rocky offshore; cottage-type accommodation in medium-low price range; handy for visiting eastern Bali and the mountains. (See page 54)

Lovina Beach: on the north coast, farthest from the airport; a long stretch of black (actually dark grey) sand; shallow water; low- to mid-priced accommodation and a scattering of restaurants; a base for diving and visits to the mountains. (See pages 63-64)

Senggigi Beach, **Lombok**: the prime place to stay in Lombok. There is an assortment of accommodation, shops, and restaurants along 10-km (6-mile) strip of coast. Beach shelves steeply in places with coral reef or rocks just below surface. (See page 77) examples of ritual and domestic items and some archaeological relics, but very few dates are given and any English labelling is more comical than informative.

Built recently, mainly out of white coral, the temple adjoining the museum compound is **Pura Jagatnata**, dedicated to Sanghyang Widi, the Supreme God. Of the many Hindu gods, the trinity of Brahma, Vishnu, and Shiva is considered to be pre-eminent, but a single god of whom all others are manifestations ties in conveniently with the Indonesian *pancasila,* or national code.

Even St. Joseph's Catholic Church in Denpasar looks more like a Balinese temple.

The tiny Catholic community attends **St. Joseph's Church** on Jalan Kepundung, off Jalan Surapati, a building thatched with palm fronds and with six distinctly Balinese-looking angels carved in stone standing above the door.

If you arrive by *bemo* from Sanur or Ubud, you'll probably alight at **Kereneng** (or Kreneng) just off the extension of Jalan Surapati, called Jalan Hayam Wuruk. (The *bemo* station for Kuta is at Tegal, southwest of the centre.)

The imposing **Arts Centre**, in spacious gardens off Jalan Nusa Indah at Abiankapas, some way out to the east, has a permanent exhibition of paintings and woodcarvings and an arena for dance and drama. A major Arts Festival is held here every

June and July. Ask about chances to see dancers and musicians practising, as well as regular performances given for visitors. You can also see dance nearby at the Sekolah Tinggi Semi Indonesia, formerly the Indonesian Academy of Dance, and still a dance academy.

Renon in the southeast is where most government buildings are gathered, including the main post office and tourist information offices.

FROM DENPASAR TO UBUD: THE CRAFT VILLAGES

When the rajas ruled Bali, they organized the various crafts on a village basis. One would specialize in wood carving, another in weaving, and a third in basketry. Passed down through each family, today those same skills are still practised in the same places. At some time or other, you're almost bound to take the route north from Denpasar, on the way to Ubud or the east coast. The villages in the area have grown and linked up, but you can tell which one you're in by their products.

A noisy traffic junction, the village of **Batubulan** (moonstone) specializes in carving statues, friezes, and ornaments out of soft grey *paras* stone. Easily shaped, it just as easily wears away, so temple decorations last only a few decades, and there is a constant demand for replacements. Bug-eyed demons line the street and Batubulan's temple is naturally a showcase. The *barong* dance (see page 88), staged every morning here, is a totally commercial production attended by busloads of tourists. Taman Barung Bah Bird Park, just north of Batubulan, is a well-arranged exhibit of exotic birds and the famous Indonesian Komodo dragon lizards.

Stop in nearby **Sukawati** for wind-chimes, puppets, basketry, ceremonial umbrellas, and jewellery. Many stalls have been brought together in the big Art Market building.

Celuk, between Ubud and Denpasar, is the base of some hundreds of silversmiths and goldsmiths, their shops and workplaces side by side along the main road and down every *gang*. They can produce any style from ornate pieces with semi-precious stones, copies of Italian fashion jewellery, to delicate filigree work in modern designs. Tour buses make a regular stop at one of the big galleries, but prices should be lower off the main road.

The Pasar Badung market in the capital city of Denpasar opens before dawn.

Like Ubud, **Batuan** developed a distinctive painting style in the 1930s when Western techniques influenced the local artists (see page 44). Dark forest green and black predominate in the early Batuan pictures, relieved by flashes of white and amber. The village is still a centre for art: painters today feature surfers and photographers, as well as Jeep-loads of tourists among the massed figures in their pictures. The main temple, Pura Desa Batuan, is especially lavishly decorated with carvings.

A short diversion eastwards will bring you to **Blahbatuh**, where the palace compound, Puri Blahbatuh, has turned into a commercial orchid nursery, sometimes referred to as Puri Anggrek (Orchid Palace).

Nearby, **Belega** specializes in bamboo, producing massive pieces of furniture. You'll see them on display along the main street, and also in use in some of Bali's hotels. Then comes **Bona**, a centre of basketry which also bills itself as the home of the *kecak* dance. The regular performances here are certainly more complete than most versions.

Back on the road to Ubud: **Mas** is famous for its wood-carvers and mask-carvers. Vast numbers of shops and work-shops line the long main street. Unless a shop has been specifically recommended, just stop anywhere and look inside, without buying right away. Then investigate the side streets. Away from the traffic, you might find an entire family producing wooden hangings for the export market.

Ubud

Once a magnet for foreign artists and still home to some, Ubud and the cluster of villages around it form the cultural focus of Bali. An increasing number of visitors come on day trips from the coastal resorts, but since morning and evening are the best times, a better plan is to stay overnight. There's a wide choice of accommodation, including cheap homestays for the budget-conscious traveller, pretty cottage-style hotels, and a handful of high-priced luxury hideaways.

Don't be too shocked by the commercialism and chaos in the main streets. Just a short walk away, you're among rice terraces suspended giddily on the sides of deep valleys.

For schedules of dance performances and other events in the vicinity, pay an early visit to the Bina Wisata information office in the middle of town. Craft stalls are packed into an ugly concrete market building on the same street. For a crash course in Balinese painting, it is certainly worthwhile visiting two museums in the town.

Museum Puri Lukisan is reached by a gateway across the road from the tourist office. In lush gardens, a fine hall has been built to house the main collection of paintings and sculpture. Look for the work of I Gusti Nyoman Lempad, one of the first artists to adopt Western techniques and bring the flat *wayang* figures of traditional painting to life. Remarkably, he was probably over 50 years old when he met Spies and Bonnet (see page 44). Even he did not know his exact age, and the museum's estimate that he died in 1978 at the age of 115 may be an exaggeration.

The superb **Museum Neka**, 2 km (1½ miles) out of town to the north of Campuhan, was founded by a local dealer and collector, Suteja Neka. In four galleries you can see the work of the Europeans who were

Balinese paintings may show scenes of rural life, like this one in the Museum Puri Lukisan.

so influential, as well as that of the finest local artists.

Some of the most striking pictures are by Indonesians working in a purely Western idiom. While others were creating new Balinese styles, they whole-heartedly adopted Western ways: only in their subject matter do these so-called "Academic painters" reveal their origins. Look for Dullah's portraits, and the *Mutual Attraction* by Abdul Aziz, where the two young figures seem to be leaning out of their frames. A photo gallery features prints of dance and everyday life in Bali in the 1930s.

Near Ubud: West and North

At the western end of town, an old suspension bridge and a new road bridge cross the Campuhan river. On the north side of the ravine is the temple of **Pura Gunung Labah**, which may date from the 8th century A.D., possibly making it one of Bali's earliest. Shrouded in dense vegetation, it overlooks Goa Raksasa, a cave named after the evil giant who is said to have dwelt there.

Just north of the Campuhan bridges, the Tjampuhan Hotel (the same place-name but in the old spelling) stands where Walter Spies (see box below) came to live in the 1930s. Across the road and up the hill, stone stairs lead to rice paddies and the track to the home of the Young Artists group at **Penestanan**. Continue your walk to **Sayan**, where Westerners have built their homes overlooking the Ayung gorge, and make your way via the rice terraces to the river.

The road from Campuhan past the Museum Neka leads to the town of **Kedewatan**, where the most luxurious hotels in the area compete to offer similarly stunning views into the Ayung valley. North of here, on one day in three, the lively morning market takes up most of the main street of **Payangan,** and it's one-way traffic for the duration. Beyond Payangan, the little-used road wends its way through scenic countryside all the way to Batur (see page 57).

Balinese Painting

When the royal court moved from Gelgel to Klungkung in the 17th century, painters from the nearby village of Kamasan were brought in to decorate the new ceremonial pavilions with scenes using mainly red, ochre, white, black, and brown.

The example of Western artists who came to live in Bali led local painters to try something new. Two who settled in Ubud in the 1930s, Walter Spies and Rudolf Bonnet, were the most influential, teaching perspective, shading, correct anatomy—everything that was lacking in the Kamasan tradition. Ubud's artists began to produce busy scenes of everyday life with naturalistic figures set against dense vegetation. When the world thinks of Balinese paintings, this is the style that comes to mind, reminding some people of the work of Rousseau.

Try to be in **Petulu**, 6 km (4 miles) north of Ubud, by about 4:00 P.M. Every evening, at sunset, thousands of white herons return from a day's fishing in the rice paddies and glide in to nest in the trees.

Southern Outskirts of Ubud

Off the main street near the information office, Monkey Forest Road heads south past lines of homestays and restaurants. After 1.8 km (1.1 miles) it reaches a small area of old trees, the home of hordes of grey monkeys. Don't provoke them— a bite can be dangerous. A fee is charged for the doubtful privilege of a visit—making monkeys out of the tourists has been a local source of amusement and income for years.

Peliatan is known for its dances and gamelan music as well as painting and carving—"parasite carvings" (see page 90) are a recent speciality. The Agong Rai Gallery sells some of the best and most expensive of modern Balinese painting.

At **Pengosekan**, just a short walk farther south, the painters concentrate on images of birds and butterflies in idyllic "Garden of Eden" landscapes. The recently opened Agong Rai Museum of Art displays Indonesian and European paintings.

EAST OF UBUD

Some of Bali's most impressive historic sites are concentrated in two small areas: one close to Ubud, another roughly 13 km (8

A doorway at the Museum Neka.

miles) away to the northeast, near Tampaksiring. Visiting them both can be easily combined in two days' touring, but inevitably, others will have the same idea. Go early if you can, to beat the crowds as well as the heat.

Goa Gajah

Closest to Ubud is the so-called **Elephant Cave**, cut into the hillside below the road just east of Teges. It probably dates from the 10th century A.D., but the whole site was buried beneath volcanic ash and mud. When the cave mouth was rediscovered in 1923, the huge face carved round it was mistaken for an elephant's head and the name has stuck. Inside the mouth, a passage measuring 12 meters (39 feet) long leads to a plain transverse chamber reaching 3.5 meters (11 feet) wide, 20 meters (66 feet) long, and high enough to stand up in. Dim electric lights reveal niches at either end that are believed to have housed shrines: one now holds a damaged statue of the elephant-headed god, Ganesha.

Later excavations revealed an 11th-century bathing pool on the terrace in front of the cave, with fountains in the shape of seven nymphs representing India's great rivers. A fairly steep scramble down the bank behind the pool leads to another cave with two ancient statues of Buddha.

Yeh Pulu

Less than 1 km (about half a mile) east of Goa Gajah, look for a signpost to **Yeh Pulu** pointing to the right, down a quiet village street. The road soon ends, but a footpath continues through rice terraces and past the local bathing pool. The rock face on the left of the path is carved in a series of scenes about 25 meters (82 feet) long. Quite different from the usual Balinese style, the simple, bold, and naturalistic figures include a prince and his servants out hunting wild boar with a woman clinging to his horse. The carvings probably date from the 14th century, but, like Goa Gajah, the site was covered by mud and only excavated in the 1920s.

Pejeng

North of Yeh Pulu and the village of Bedulu, the archaeological museum **Parbakala Gedong Arca** brings together the neolithic and Bronze Age relics unearthed in this area, which include stone sarcophagi dating from about 500 B.C. The exhibits are neither well organized nor labelled but, as this is also a study centre, you may be lucky and have someone knowledgeable on hand.

The entrance to Pura Kebo Edan, a temple boasting a 10-foot statue of Bima.

Several temples in the area are worth a short stop. **Pura Kebo Edan** has a statue of the giant Bima, standing 3 meters (10 feet) tall, with multiple penises, trampling on a copulating couple. A collection of ancient statuary includes some dating from the 13th century. There's more fine carved stonework at the 14th-century Pura Pusering Jagat, known as the "Temple of the Navel of the World." During full moon, childless couples pray at the stone shrines depicting *lingam* and *yoni* (male and female genitalia).

At **Pura Penataran Sasih**, a great hollow bronze drum cast in one piece and 1.5 meters (5 feet) across, stands high up on a platform at the back of the temple. The style is typical of the Dong-son Bronze Age dynasty of Vietnam dating from about 300 B.C., but whether it was brought to Bali or made here is unknown. According to legend, it fell from the sky. A section has been broken out of it at some time, and only the geometric patterns are visible from ground level: decoration not in view includes faces with staring eyes.

Tampaksiring

To the north of Pejeng Region the road climbs for 10 km (6 miles) to Tampaksiring, where craft shops compete to entice tour buses to stop on their way to Batur (see page 57). In the middle of the long village street, look for a sign pointing down a road to the right to **Gunung Kawi**, 1.5 km (1 mile) away. A long flight of steps descending into a valley is lined by stalls selling bright sarongs, carved coconut shells, and cold drinks. If you don't buy a drink on the way down, the drinks vendors can afford to be patient: hot, thirsty, and tired tourists toiling back up are a captive market.

At the bottom of the steps, a narrow passage and gateway cut through solid rock and then open out suddenly into the temple area. Round to the left, two rows of hollows have been carved out of the cliffs on either side of a ravine. Legend says they're the marks of a giant's fingernails, scraped out in a single night. (The head of the giant, Kebo Iwa, is carved out in stone at Pura Gadun, in Blahbatuh; see page 41.) The rock was sculpted so as to leave a *candi* (shrine) measuring 7 meters (23 feet) in each hollow, believed to be some 11th-century memorials to a royal dynasty.

Not to be confused with the place Gunung Kawi, the temple of **Pura Gunung Kawi** is some way away in the village of Sebatu, and often many visitors asking for directions have been sent there by mistake. In fact, it is worth the trip, partly for the sights and scenery en route. From Tampaksiring the road opposite the turning to Tirta Empul twists through villages which specialize in the mass production of woodcarvings. You'll see rows of identical ducks alongside armies of chess pieces and perhaps some original new design of statue that hasn't yet hit any of the shops. Two successive right turns, signposted, lead to Sebatu and Pura Gunung Kawi, a brightly painted temple with sacred springs feeding water to ponds and bathing pools.

At the northern edge of Tampaksiring, the road forks right. Immediately on the left is the temple and holy spring of **Tirta Empul**, source of the river that flows through Gunung Kawi. It is believed to have been created by the god Indra to revive his ailing army, whose men had been poisoned by an enemy. He pierced the earth, and out flowed *amerta*, the water of immortality. It is still thought by many to have healing powers, and the pools here are often thronged with those seeking purification. The temple is sited against a wooded hillside, in contrast to the nearby souvenir

The giant rock-cut candis at Gunung Kawi were carved about a thousand years ago.

shops, which are as ugly as any in Bali. High above the temple stands a government rest house built by the Dutch and turned into a palace by the late President Sukarno, who they say kept a telescope trained on the women's pool.

EASTERN BALI

In contrast to the softer south, here the mountain slopes reach down to the sea, creating rocky shores and small bays. Where there is sand, it's grey, the result of the weathering of old lava. The rajas once ruled most of Bali from their capitals at Karangasem (now Amlapura) and Klungkung. Approaching from the south, the road passes through busy **Gianyar**, also a former raja's capital. The brick palace in the centre of town is still the home of his family and not open to the public. Weaving is the main industry, and a number of small factories as well as some workshops along the road from Ubud are open for tours. Here you can learn about making *ikat* (*endek* in Balinese), using threads that have been tie-dyed in bunches before weaving.

Near **Sidan**, 3 km (2 miles) east of Gianyar, stone friezes with scary demons carved out of them cover the walls of the Pura Dalem, the temple of the dead, situated by the roadside overlooking rice terraces.

Klungkung

The dynasty founded by Batu Renggong, the first Dewa Agung, was paramount in Bali for 300 years, first ruling from Gelgel and then moving to Klungkung in 1710. Standing high above the modern town where its broad main streets cross, **Kerta Gosa**, the Royal Hall of Justice, was built at the time of the move and continued as a courthouse under the Dutch. The ceiling is covered in vivid paintings in a style unique to the region. Although the paintings have frequently been restored and in fact entirely replaced more than once, the work has always been done by artists from the nearby village of Kamasan, and it is likely that the designs resemble the 18th-century originals. Many of the panels relate tales from Balinese mythology, but visitors' eyes tend to be drawn to the series depicting the dreadful punishments awaiting evildoers in the kingdom of the dead.

Important guests were received in the **Bale Kambang**, a pavilion surrounded by water to give the appearance of floating among the water lilies. Its painted ceiling illustrates more stories from Balinese legend, without the gory details. Facing the palace garden, a small **museum** has been opened in one of the old buildings. Some of the most impressive exhibits are the photographs of the rajas and their families, dating from before 1908, the year of the *puputan* which took place in the open space in front of the palace and marked the end of effective resistance to the Dutch (see page 21). Across the street, a monument erected in 1992 commemorates that tragic event.

In **Kamasan**, only 2 km (1½ miles) south of Klungkung, painters are still working in the classical style seen on the Kerta Gosa ceiling. Take a left turn to find their studios. The former royal capital of **Gelgel**, farther along, is now no more than a prosperous village.

West of Klungkung, a narrow lane leads to the village of **Tihingan**, one of only two places in Bali where the gongs are made for gamelan orchestras. The other is Sawan, near the north coast (see page 65). In any of the bronze foundries, you'll find the same medieval scene, with a boy apprentice pumping the bellows to keep a charcoal fire blazing while the smiths hammer away. Hanging mats keep the place in semi-darkness so that the workers can judge the temperature of the glowing metal by its colour. In the village of Banda, about 5 km (3 miles) south of Tihinga, a new museum celebrates one of Bali's most successful contemporary artists, Nyoman Gunarsa.

On the eastern periphery of Klungkung a bridge crosses the gorge of the Unda river, which is used as a big communal bath every afternoon as the sun goes down. Ash, mud, and floods from the 1963 eruption of Gunung Agung devastated this part of the island, and the effects are still felt today, as its agriculture has not yet fully recovered from the disaster.

The main road meets the sea at **Kusamba**, a partly Muslim fishing village. Look out for the sign to Pasar Ikan (the fish market) situated at the eastern end, where a few sharks or tuna are sliced up for sale. Across a dirty stream, dozens of outrigger boats are hauled up on the black sandy beach. Some of them sail from here to the offshore island of **Nusa Penida**, the larger neighbour of Nusa Lembongan (see page 29). Nusa Penida's dry climate and limestone cliffs have more in common with the Bukit Peninsula than the rest of Bali. The beaches of the island's north shore are edged by pens used for growing edible seaweed—look out for the strange patterns if you are flying between Bali and Lombok.

Wayang art at Gelgel, original seat of power of the first Dewa Agung.

Goa Lawah

Considered one of Bali's oddities, the **Bat Cave** and its temple are hemmed in by souvenir stalls, hawkers, sash dispensers, donation collectors, ticket sellers, and, for most of the day, by parked tour buses. Once past this obstacle course, you'll see the cave mouth and a seething mass of leathery bats clinging to the rock face, here and there dropping off, circling and then coming in to land again. They can't all find a place in the cave, so some hang outside in broad daylight. If you are staying anywhere near, perhaps at Candi Dasa, you might time a visit here for dusk. That's when the bat colony pours out of the cave like a liquid black stream and wheels away into the distance to feed on the myriad insects of the tropical night. Bats are part of the evening scene in Bali, flitting through the trees as soon as the sun sets. Don't be surprised if a bat makes a low swoop over your dinner table, whether in the local café or at a luxury resort.

On the foreshore near the Bat Cave, a few people scratch a living by harvesting salt. Seawater is first concentrated by solar evaporation in shallow pans and then transferred to the hollowed-out halves of palm tree trunks to crystallize.

Padangbai

This little port stands on Bali's only natural harbour with an unobstructed approach from the sea. The first Dutch ships dropped anchor in the sheltered bay in 1597 (see page 17). Today's cruise ships usually do the same, and their passengers are ferried ashore for sight-seeing excursions.

A regular passenger and car ferry makes two or three sailings per day to Lombok. The voyage can be rough and may take longer than the scheduled four hours. Many visitors opt for the newer, faster, and more expensive twin-hull ferry from Benoa Port (see page 35), but backpackers and most locals stay faithful to the old route. If you plan to use the ferry, take measures against seasickness. The first-class section offers shade, but on the upper deck you'll need a hat and sunblock. Food and drink are sold on board.

Fishermen land their catches consisting of tuna, barracuda, and sometimes even a shark, at Padangbai's small busy beach, jammed with boats, just to the north of the main jetty. Facing it at the far end are two or three simple but adequate cottage-style homestays. You can arrange diving or fishing trips here, but the water in the bay looks too dirty for swimming.

Beyond Padangbai comes the broad sweep of Amuk Bay, site of a controversial new oil terminal. At its eastern end, after the coast road crosses an iron bridge, a track leads down to the sea at the village of Buitan, also called **Balina Beach**, the name of its main hotel and scuba-diving centre.

Candi Dasa

Cottage-style hotels and homestays began to be built along this stretch of coast in the early 1980s. People in search of more quiet than Kuta and lower prices than Sanur and Nusa Dua offered them liked the easy-going atmosphere, the beach of grey volcanic sand, and snorkelling over the reef. Then came a setback. For many years, villagers had been chipping away at the offshore reef and using the coral to make lime for building purposes. In places it collapsed, the beach it had protected slowly began to be washed away, and the foreshore was eroded. In an attempt to stem the loss, ugly concrete blocks were dropped into the sea. It's impossible to say if they have had any positive effect. Hopes of reversing the erosion have certainly been dashed. There's still some dark sand exposed during low tide, mixed with broken coral, so it is advisable to wear shoes.

There's a lot to be said for the slow-down of development at Candi Dasa. It has remained fairly low-key, with reasonable prices. Tranquil little Balinese bungalows under the palm trees are just what many visitors are looking for.

In an island of varied villages, **Tenganan** is one of the strangest. From Candi Dasa, it is 4 km (2½ miles) inland, on the lower slopes of Mount Agung. The residents there are Bali Aga, "original Balinese," and many of their customs and rituals date from the animist days before the advent of Hinduism. They have their own music and dances. Marriage outside the community used to be forbidden, and the population shrank. Once the rule was eased, the trend halted.

The rough road from the coast terminates at a parking area outside the village walls, where you are asked to make a donation before entering. One long street climbs up from the main gateway, past a succession of open-sided pavilions and up cobblestoned terraces. By day it becomes a continuous market, with some unusually chatty as well as cheerful shopkeepers. The weavers of Tenganan are well known for making *grinsing* (or *gerinsing*) cloth, a double *ikat* (see page 92) in which both warp and weft threads are tie-dyed in bunches before weaving. The intricacy of the process of lining up the patterns can only be imagined: it takes months to make a sarong and prices are high. You'll see a lot of cloth that is fake—the genuine item is rare.

Amlapura (Karangasem)

North of Candi Dasa the road turns inland, crossing hills and fertile valleys, with views of the volcanic cone of Gunung Agung. Amlapura was known as Karangasem before 1963. That is still the name of the region, but its capital wanted to erase the memory of Mount Agung's eruption and perhaps to deceive any evil spirits into sparing it the next time. Part of the raja's palace and gardens were damaged then, but there has been some restoration, and one of three palaces at the site, Puri Agung, is open to visitors.

The last raja fancied his talents as an architect and built two rather elaborate water gardens. **Ujung** on the coast was built in the 1920s. It was devastated in 1963 but some of its gateways, pavilions, terraces, and its weed-choked pool still stand, forlorn and deserted, like the relics of some far more ancient civilization.

From Ujung, a coast road skirts the eastern tip of Bali, but it is potholed and crosses many river beds, usually dry but impassable after heavy rain. The scenery is not varied enough to make the bumpy two-hour ride to Amed worth the effort. In any case, there's a much more beautiful alternative—taking in the raja's second fancy creation, the water playground in the hills at **Tirtagangga** 5 km (3 miles) northwest of Amlapura. This one was only established after World War II, and despite being nearer to the eruption, it was spared serious damage. You can cool off in the spring-fed pools built for the raja's family, and there are

You are welcome to cool off in the pools of a former raja's water garden at Tirtagangga.

places to stay if you want to enjoy the refreshing air and magical dawn light. One *losmen* is inside the water garden area.

On the road north, a right fork at Culik leads eastwards to **Amed**, where a stretch of the shore is given over to salt pans and hollowed-out palm trunks used for seawater evaporation. An alternative to the north-coast way is to head west to **Sibetan** past the rice fields shining with shades of green.

THE MOUNTAINS

To the Balinese, the mountains are the abode of the gods, the source of the rivers that water their crops, and of occasional outbursts of destructive fury. The highest of them are active or dormant volcanoes: Gunung Batur simmers more or less continuously while Gunung Agung erupts violently once every few hundred years. When you set out for the higher altitudes, go prepared for it to be cold, with damp mists, or for scorching sunshine. Many tour companies run day trips, sometimes combining visits to Besakih (see page 60) and Penelokan (see page 58). This is an easy way to see the views, but you will arrive at the same time as hundreds of others. With more and more accommodation opening, think about overnighting at a mountain resort, or somewhere cheaper. If you plan to climb one of the peaks—not a mountaineering feat but a few hours' or a full day's hill walking and scrambling over rocks—it's essential to stay nearby and start early.

Bangli

On the main road from the south towards Mount Batur, the chief town of the former rajadom of Bangli looks like a nursery for gorgeous flowering shrubs. It comes alive every three days for the big morning market in the central square. To the south of town on the Gianyar road is Pura Dalem Penuggekan, a typical example of the many temples for the dead: carved friezes show the nightmarish tortures awaiting sinners in the after-life. On the northern outskirts, the chief temple of the former rajadom of Bangli, Pura Kehen, comprises the typical three courtyards, here particularly large and linked by steep flights of steps. The walls of the first were once encrusted with inset porcelain plates, but many have been broken or lost.

Around Lake Batur

The roads from the south climb out of the rice paddies of the lowlands, through coffee plantations and orchards at around 600

Locals pose in a dug-out canoe at Lake Batur, but in general they don't like to be photographed.

meters (2,000 feet), eventually thinning out into open pasture. A band of rainforest blocks out the view until you emerge at 1,300 meters (4,300 feet) on the narrow rim of a huge crater (technically a *caldera* or collapsed volcano), 11 km (7 miles) across and about 200 meters (660 feet) deep. The pastel blue crescent of Lake Batur takes up the eastern third of the great bowl, and out of the centre grows Mount Batur itself, bare rock streaked with black traces of old lava flows. **Penelokan** ("Place for Looking") can offer a great panorama, but it's an ugly village, at its worst when enveloped in a cold wet fog and you can't see the view anyway. The pedlars here are especially pressing, and that's nothing new: Balinese travellers have complained about them since long before the arrival of tourists. The height of confusion comes at lunchtime when the tour buses disgorge their passengers at the restaurants especially built for them.

There's an even better view into the *caldera*, and no fuss, from the road a short way east from Penelokan (heading towards Suter and Rendang, the turnoff for Besakih).

Mount Batur went into an active phase in August 1994, blowing huge puffs of smoke and rocky debris from a new vent on its northwest face. As a result, some of the tracks there were cut. It is best always to seek local advice before you contemplate venturing up the mountain.

A steep zig-zag road winds down to the lake: *bemos* and motorcycle jockeys are ready to take anyone without transport to **Kedisan**, a lakeside village where you will find a few modest homestays.

Trunyan, on the eastern shore and usually reached by boat from Kedisan, is a Bali Aga (original Balinese) village but, unlike Tenganan (see page 54), this one is far from picturesque or friendly.

On the lake's western shore, reached by a road winding through lava fields, lies **Tirta**, or **Toyabungkah**, known for its hot springs. They are naturally accounted both holy and highly therapeutic, and channelled into a public pool —as hot as a steaming bath. You can also enjoy the thermal waters at a new spa complex in the center of town. A scattering of homestays and rudimentary eating places has now been dwarfed by a big hotel resembling a Chinese palace, with its own fibreglass "rock" pool fed by hot spring water.

Tirta makes a good base for the two-hour climb (longer in the heat of the day) to the summit of Mount Batur. It's best to start before dawn: some of the guided parties set out as early as 3:30 A.M. Guides, available locally or at Kintamani, can suggest various longer hikes.

Batur was rebuilt in its present position on the crater rim after a 1926 eruption buried the old site down below. One long street is lined with ugly concrete houses and sheds, relieved by Pura Ulun Danu, the new temple of black volcanic stone started in 1927 and still being extended. **Kintamani**, adjoining Batur, is brightened up only by its market, on Monday and Thursday mornings.

The road follows on to the north coast, passing close to **Gunung Peninsulan**, which is 1,745 meters (5,725 feet) high. A flight of 350 steps takes you to the summit, crowned by Bali's tallest temple, Pura Tegeh Koripan. Traces of stone structures date back to prehistoric times. At the very top, a plain walled enclosure holds a collection of beautiful stone statues and panels portraying gods and rulers, some dating from the 10th and 11th centuries. On a clear day, the views alone of the mountains and north coast make the rather strenuous climb well worth it.

Gunung Agung

Bali's highest peak, at 3,142 meters (10,309 feet), is also its holiest. Still active today, the volcano erupted in 1963 (see page 24) and poured red-hot lava down its slopes, setting villages ablaze. Ash covered much of northern Bali, ruining crops and blocking up the rivers. When they broke through, several villages and towns along their banks were inundated with mud.

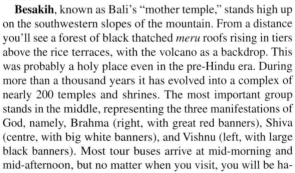

Besakih, known as Bali's "mother temple," stands high up on the southwestern slopes of the mountain. From a distance you'll see a forest of black thatched *meru* roofs rising in tiers above the rice terraces, with the volcano as a backdrop. This was probably a holy place even in the pre-Hindu era. During more than a thousand years it has evolved into a complex of nearly 200 temples and shrines. The most important group stands in the middle, representing the three manifestations of God, namely, Brahma (right, with great red banners), Shiva (centre, with big white banners), and Vishnu (left, with large black banners). Most tour buses arrive at mid-morning and mid-afternoon, but no matter when you visit, you will be harassed by hawkers and goaded by guides and ordered by gatekeepers to make donations. Local people don't see this commercial activity as inappropriate; to them, a temple isn't a holy place until the gods are present, and that only happens during a religious ceremony.

There are also guides offering their services to those who want to climb Gunung Agung; only the fit and well prepared should attempt it, and only in the dry season. Even then, the expedition can take as long as twelve hours and involves a lot of slipping and sliding on unpleasant stony slopes.

Bedugul

The direct road from Denpasar to Singaraja traverses some of Bali's prettiest hill country, with views of dormant volcanoes and three crater lakes. At about 1,300 meters (4,300 feet), the spring-like climate has made Bedugul—the village has lent its name to the whole area—into something of a mountain retreat. The Botanic Gardens and orchid nurseries are both at their best in the rainy season and make an agreeable place for a stroll or a picnic at any time. **Bukit Mungsu** market nearby is bright with flowers and superb fruit, especially the local passionfruit. There are watersports facilities on **Lake Beratan** (or Bratan), while the lakeside temple of Ulu Danu at **Candikuning** ranks as one of Bali's most photogenic. (Its final courtyard is right out in the lake.) **Pancasari** has a variety of attractive cottage-style hotels, and the views of the mountainside towering above Lake Buyan in the distance, seen from the championship golf course at **Bali Handara Kosaido Country Club**, are superb. The road winds its way up to the old crater rim above the lake. You will find monkeys congregating wherever you decide to stop and look at the view. Once you've reached the top there's a choice of routes to the north coast. The main road descends by way of bamboo forest and banana plantations direct to Singaraja. Alternatively, you can take the little-used back road past lakes Buyan and Tamblingan and down through **Munduk** to Seririt (see page 66). The remote hillside villages specialize in growing cloves, and you will see as well as smell carpets of the pink buds laid out by the roadside to dry. A new attraction in Munduk is the so-called Pyramid Plastic, built from melted plastic waste as a reminder of the environmental damage that tourism and industry is causing in Bali.

THE NORTH COAST

Before the days of flying, most visitors to Bali arrived in the north. The first Dutch military expeditions disembarked near Singaraja, which became the island's administrative capital and the colony's chief port. Now, almost everyone arrives and stays in southern Bali, and only a fraction of them ever take a trip to the north coast, although the journey takes less than two hours by road.

There is quite a contrast between the south and north. It is hotter and drier in the north and far less densely populated. The proportion of Muslims is higher; some of the people are descended from traders and immigrants from other islands. There is only a narrow strip of flat land between the mountains and the sea, or in places none at all. Cactus plants are as common as palm trees and the small area of rice depends on irrigation.

Lacking an airport, losing the status of capital, and denied any substantial cash flow from tourism, **Singaraja** hasn't expanded as much as Denpasar. As can be expected from the former capital, colonial buildings predominate in the port area of **Bululeng** (the original town that gave its name to the northern rajadom) and the old centre. Pleasant garden suburbs, formerly home to the Dutch administrators, straggle inland up the hills. But there's little to detain a visitor and no attractive accommodation. For that, you have to travel a short distance out of town.

Lovina Beach

The beaches west of Singaraja began to attract escapist travellers in the early 1970s, and simple and fairly inexpensive accommodation was built to house

Fishing boats picturesquely litter Bali's beaches.

them. Slowly the number of visitors grew and the small homestays turned themselves into larger bungalow-type hotels. Today, tour groups come for short stays and, as everywhere in Bali, standards and prices are steadily going up. Actually, Lovina is not one village but a string of small ones, starting 6 km (4 miles) west of Singaraja and continuing for 10 km (6 miles) up the coast road. Shops, restaurants, and moneychangers are scattered along the busy stretch.

The beach itself is shallow and gently shelving, making it an ideal place for small children. There is calm water on the inside of the reef and good snorkelling over it. Lovina's dark sand is less inviting than the white or golden variety at the southern resorts, and gets too hot to walk on in bare feet in the middle of the day.

Balinese women dress their smartest to take offerings to one of the village temples.

Dawn and dusk are the best times. Dolphins frolic offshore almost every morning—boats will take you out to see them close up. At sunset, the fishermen prepare for a night's work aided by batteries of lights on the boats to attract their catch while local farmers herd their goats or lead their water buffaloes along the sand. If you're lucky, you may be around to see the races between beautifully decorated pairs of water buffaloes pulling a sled round a track in the fields. Ask if any are scheduled: they follow the Balinese calendar.

East of Singaraja

Once clear of the outskirts of the town, at **Sangsit**, look for a turn off the main road (there will be signs), heading towards the sea, to the beautiful temple of **Pura Beji**. Dedicated to the rice goddess, this is the most elaborate and ornate temple in the north. It's decorated with intricate carvings of flowers and animals, gods, and monsters.

The road that leads inland for 5 km (3 miles) will take you to **Jagaraga**, a village fortified by Jelantik against the Dutch colonialists in 1848 and 1849. The small temple on the left-hand side just before you reach the village centre has some of the strangest carved stone decoration in Bali—and some of the most secular, dating from the 1930s. In one panel, an open-top car carries two European passengers being held up by a man with a gun, while others point up at some aeroplanes—one of them crashing into the sea. Jagaraga is also famous for its dance troupes, which can sometimes be seen in performance here.

About 2 km (1½ miles) to the south of Jagaraga, **Sawan** has a couple of gongmakers' workshops that supply gamelan orchestras: the only other village where the craft is practised is in Tihingan situated near Klungkung (see page 51). Methods are utterly traditional. Bronze is made by melting copper and tin together by heating them in an ancient pot over red-hot charcoal, or else old and broken instruments are re-cycled. The molten bronze is poured into stone moulds to form rough discs, which are then hammered and heated and hammered again until they finally take the shape of gongs. It's essential that the craftsmen who make the gongs have a musical ear so they are able to ensure that the sets of gongs are suitable for the five-tone Balinese scale. The correct note is ensured by adjusting the mass of metal and its distribution over the surface of the gong.

Back on the coast road at **Kumbutambahan,** in the temple of Pura Maduwe Karang, you'll find a famous carving of a man on a bicycle, its wheels taking the form of flowers. To the east, at **Air Sanih** (or Yeh Sanih), you can join local people bathing in the pools fed by a natural spring and shaded by the palm trees. A few simple tourist bungalows have been built at the site.

The often empty coast road continues past Tianyar to Tulamben, renowned for superb snorkelling and diving on the submerged wreck of the U.S. cargo ship *Liberty*, which sank here in World War II.

For information on the eastern tip of Bali, see page 50.

West of Singaraja

At Dencarik, to the west of Lovina, the road inland climbs a steep hill before reaching the orange-roofed building of the **Buddhist monastery** known as Brahma Vihara Arama. Nearby, at **Banjar Tega**, the warm springs (signposted *Air Panas*) have been piped into a public swimming pool, attractively shaded. There are a smaller and hotter pool, a natural shower, and reasonably clean changing rooms.

The market town of **Seririt** is a busy junction with one road leading across the island to Tabenan and eventually to Denpasar and the other following the coastal route westward. Celukanbawang Bay, 12 km (7 miles) from Seririt, is likely to become an important port if development plans are realized. So far there's a wharf, but rarely a ship to be seen. After about another 25 km (16 miles) of sparsely settled shoreline, you'll come to **Pura Pulaki**, an important temple recently rebuilt out of grim, black volcanic stone and frequented by hundreds of monkeys. Traces remain of older parts of the temple carved out of the cliff face, a natural aggregate of volcanic debris which quickly wears away — the pebbly beach here is the result.

A large part of this end of the island has been designated as the **West Bali National Park**, and the road crosses a small section of it, an area covered with woodland and scrub, with plenty of grey monkeys. True rainforest extends over the park's southern slopes.

Labuhan Lalang on Terima Bay is the base for boats which make the half-hour trip to **Pulau Menjangan** (Deer Island). Mainly scrub-covered and only 3 km (2 miles) long, Labuhan Lalang's coral reefs and clear water are highly rated among scuba divers.

Across the western tip of Bali, mangrove swamps surround **Gilimanuk**, not much more than one wide street, a few homestays, and the ferry terminal for Java. The silhouette of Gunung Merapi, still an active volcano, is often visible in the mist across the water.

WEST OF DENPASAR

Fertile land and high rainfall have brought prosperity to this part of Bali, without the debatable benefits of tourism. In the main towns, you'll find more computer suppliers than souvenir shops. There is very little in the way of accommodation and not much choice when it comes to eating, but the region is rewarding to explore.

The back roads are quiet: only the main highway west is heavily used. There's no coast road for about the first 50 km (30 miles) or so, and all traffic is funnelled through **Kapal**, where the main industry is making cement castings, from kitsch ornaments to concrete pipes. Here you can buy all the pieces for an off-the-peg temple, complete with a *meru* (a shrine which usually has multiple pagoda roofs). This industry developed from a tradition of stone carving, and naturally the local temple, Pura Sadha, believed to date back to the 12th century, is intricately embellished.

Mengwi

Just to the northwest of Kapal, there's a major road junction. The right fork goes north to Bedugul (see page 61) and Singaraja, but you only have to go 3 km (2 miles) to reach Mengwi, and also one of Bali's most beautiful temples.

A right turn in the town centre leads immediately to **Pura Taman Ayun**. Built in 1634 and renovated in 1937, it's notable for a double moat. Every morning as well as late in the afternoon, people use the wide outer moat for washing themselves and their clothes. You can circle the outside of the wall that surrounds the inner compound and look in at the cluster of *merus* (shrines with pagodas), with any odd number of thatched roofs.

Once the daily influx of visitors begins, about mid-morning, an outrigger boat shuttles people across the outer moat to a craft display and shop.

North of Mengwi (signposted, situated off the main road) is **Sangeh Monkey Forest**, a grove of tall nutmeg trees protected for their religious significance and also as a nature reserve. The residents engage in their business swinging from branch to branch and flock to Bukit Sari, the temple, while hawkers swarm round the visitors. Remember to hide all portable possessions from the monkeys.

Those in the mood to explore should head north from Sangeh, where the road climbs into lovely countryside and rarely visited villages. Eventually it peters out on the slopes of Mount Catur.

Lovina on the north coast is a succession of dark sand beaches, sheltered by reefs.

Marga

In November 1946, Ngurah Rai and his men were trapped by Dutch forces close to this village, 12 km (7 miles) northwest of Mengwi. In an heroic but hopeless last stand, they were all killed (see page 22). The battlefield just north of the village is now marked by several memorials. A statue depicts a group of defiant freedom fighters. The Margarana monument is a tall *candi* (or shrine) whose columns carry the symbols of *pancasila*, the five principles of the Indonesian state (see page 23). Carved panels record Ngurah Rai's message to the Dutch, demanding their withdrawal and ending with the words "*Sekali Merdeka, Tetap Merdeka*" (or "Freedom now, freedom forever"). Beyond the shrine is a field of memorials to all those who died for the cause of Bali's independence— in total 1,372 men and women. It looks like a cemetery, but these are not actual graves.The museum at the site is worth a visit for the photographs and other relics of the campaign.

If you have reliable transport and a good road map, head farther north into the hills for 16 km (10 miles) along little-used roads to **Pura Luhur**, the chief temple of the rajadom of Tabenan, beautifully set amid lush forest. Despite its ancient appearance, this is a modern reconstruction—lichens grow quickly in the high humidity.

Tanah Lot

Practically every brochure for Bali shows this sea temple on its rocky islet, often silhouetted against the setting sun. Inevitably, tour buses converge here in late afternoon so everyone can take that same picture. It is 10 km (6 miles) down a narrow side road from Kediri to the coast, and there can be a long procession of traffic. You might like to plan a dawn visit instead, avoiding at least some of the hawkers who congregate later in the day. Tanah Lot is believed to have been founded in the 16th century by the Javanese priest Nirarta, who dedicated it to the sea god. Now the sea threatens to undermine the rock on which it stands, and concrete breakwaters have been positioned to hold back the waves. Nothing, however, is done to hold back the commercial tide. Ever more souvenir stands and food stalls cluster as near as they can get, and the nearby coast is being developed as a huge, and controversial, resort complex.

But the former raja's capital of **Tabanan** goes about its business with few concessions to tourism. The Dutch burned the palace here in 1906, so the heart of the old town is gone, but Tabanan remains a centre for music and dance. **Kerambitan**, just off the main road to the southwest, is a pretty town with three palaces, still the property of a princely family. Today, one of the palaces, the Puri Anyar, acts as an aristocratic type of homestay, where guests can experience the traditional hospitality that might have been extended to honoured visitors in the past.

The main road reaches the coast at Soka, with two small beaches and occasional good surfing waves. **Balian Beach** is similar, with informal bungalow accommodation. Experi-

---

Getting Around Lombok

Some **organized tours** from Senggigi go to a few cultural sites and craft villages, or take you to one of the Gilis (see page 77) to snorkel or dive. **Bemos** (minivans; see page 126) run from town to town, but rarely outside the densely populated central lowland area. You can arrange to charter them for approximately the price of a rental vehicle per day. The ubiquitous **cidomo** (a pony and trap similar to Bali's dokar) is fine for short rides. **Taxis** need to be pre-arranged. **Cars** are hired at Senggigi and Mataram. **Bikes** are available for rental, and the mountains are good for **hiking**, in the dry season.

enced surfers head west to **Medewi**, where some attractive new cottage-style hotels face a mostly rocky shore with no more than a small beach.

The sea temple at **Rambut Siwi**, off the main road, stands on a black rock overlooking the sandy shore. Some attractive buildings and a profusion of flowering trees crown the cliff top.

Negara, 23 km (14 miles) farther west, is known for its water-buffalo racing. The season traditionally ran for September and October, and the championships still take place then, but races are now staged year round for the benefit of visitors on a track at Perencak, outside Negara. Tour agencies offer excursions from Kuta, Sanur, and the other resorts.

LOMBOK

Bali's smaller neighbour to the east, easily visible on a clear day, is at times billed by hopeful promoters and developers as "the next Bali." That, however, paints a misleading picture; the scenery, the people, their culture, and religion are all too different. There is less rainfall and the rainy season is prone to fail, leaving most of the island parched and dusty. It may be only a 20-minute flight away, or a few hours by ferry, but it's another world.

Not all of Bali's art is religious, as demonstrated by this relief of a man on a bicycle.

Lombok is roughly 70 km (43 miles) from north to south and the same distance across. Its one great mountain, Gunung Rinjani, is among the highest in Indonesia and dominates the northern half of the island. Most people live on the east-west plain across the middle, fertile after rain and sunscorched by the dry season. The far south is arid, with low, scrub-covered hills and eroded valleys, rather like some parts of northern Australia.

From a study of their plants and animals, the 19th-century naturalist Alfred Wallace divided the Indonesian islands into a western group, regarded as part of southeast Asia, and an eastern group, which belonged geographically to Australasia. He then drew the line between the two through the Lombok Strait separating Bali and Lombok. The division is not quite so clear-cut now, but the basic principle of the "Wallace Line" is still accepted.

For many years, the island of Lombok was the domain of the Sasaks, a people who had come from the Asian mainland by way of Java and Bali. They were animists who revered the spirits they believed to be in the living things and inanimate objects around them. As Islam spread through the islands (apart from Bali) some people in Lombok adopted it in a version of their own, Wektu Telu, which retained many influences of animism. Today, a majority of people are more or less orthodox Muslims: as you travel about Lombok, you will notice the growing numbers of young women who wear robes and headscarves.

The first succession of Balinese invasions started in the 16th century. For a while most of Lombok was governed from Karangasem in Bali: later the Balinese in Lombok were independent, and even attempted to capture Karangasem! The beliefs of the animist-Hindu Balinese and the animist-Muslim Sasaks, however, were not always in conflict; there was a lot of intermarriage. Today the Balinese minority mainly lives in west Lombok and is influential in commerce and tourism.

At the end of the 19th century, the Dutch took advantage of the conflict raging between the Sasaks and Balinese, joining in on the Sasak side and then taking complete control. After the Japanese occupied Lombok in World War II, the Dutch briefly returned, only to have to depart again when Indonesia became independent.

Where to Go in Lombok

You won't find many notable temples, palaces, or other historic sites, but Lombok visitors are rewarded in different ways: the sight of water buffaloes and their calves, hens, and chicks dashing across your path; sudden views of blue sea dotted with sails. Most visitors stay in the hotels alongside Senggigi beach, but the far south and the offshore Gilis also have good beaches and snorkelling.

Some villages are renowned for their traditional crafts —intricate basketry, weaving, pottery, or carving. A few of them have realized the chances of increasing the flow of tourist traffic, setting up stalls by the road-

The resident monkeys expect to be fed, and they'll try to take any portable property as well.

The water pool at Narmada was laid out to remind a raja of beloved mountain lakes.

side or getting younger members of the family to bring visitors to have a look at the work going on. For an insight into village life, it's worth inquiring about the timing of local market days, held in the mornings once or twice a week in many towns and villages. Roads are refreshingly free of traffic; the prime source of motive power is still tiny ponies pulling unlikely loads in two-wheeled traps.

Ampenan, Mataram, and Cakranegara

Flights land at Selaparang Airport, on the northern outskirts of Lombok's provincial capital, Mataram. The ferries from Bali dock at Lembar, 10 km (6 miles) to the south.

Not so long ago the old port of Ampenan, the administrative centre of Mataram, and the commercial district of Cakranegara were completely separate. Now they have joined up in an urban sprawl, home to a quarter of a million pcople. A long, broad avenue lined by an improbable number of government buildings links them all and then continues to Sweta, the island's transport hub.

The port area of **Ampenan** is crumbling and mostly disused, but the narrow streets of the old town are livelier. Many of the people here are descended from Arab traders —noticeable from the well-attended mosques and the noisy cries calling the faithful to prayer. A variety of so-called "antique" shops sell the odd interesting relic amid piles of dusty junk. The **museum**, which is south of the centre on Jalan Banjar Tilar Negara, gives an overview of the island's culture, as well as its unique and volatile ecology.

Mataram has the array of government institutions found in every Indonesian provincial capital, as well as tree-lined residential streets with many opulent houses. **Cakranegara** (or just Cakra—remember that it is pronounced "Chakra") grew up around the palace of the Balinese rajas. Today it is the commercial centre of Lombok. All that remains today of the royal compound is the 1744 **Mayura Water Palace**, the former meeting hall and court of justice standing in the middle of a lake and reached by a causeway guarded by old cannons. This was the scene of a short-lived Balinese victory over Dutch troops in 1894: the result was reversed only weeks later and the Dutch went on to take over the whole island.

Across the way, **Pura Meru**, the biggest temple in Lombok, was built in 1720. It has three *meru*-topped shrines dedicated to Brahma, Shiva, and Vishnu. The huge wooden drums in the outer courtyard are sounded calling the Hindu community to festivals and ceremonies. Just to the east, **Sweta** buzzes with *bemos*, buses, and pony-powered *cidomos*.

Tempering new clay pots with burning straw at Penujak in the south of Lombok.

Near the Capital

The hillside gardens and lake at **Narmada**, 10 km (6 miles) east of Cakranegara, were laid out for a 19th-century raja to remind him of Gunung Rinjani and its crater lake when he became too infirm to make the journey to the real mountain. The resemblance is harder to see now that an extra pool and a rectangular swimming pool have been added.

To the north of Narmada at **Lingsar**, a new spring is said to have burst into life to greet the Balinese when they came to Lombok, and they chose the site for an ecumenical temple intended to bring together people of different religions. The upper compound is reserved for the Hindus. The pool in the Wektu Telu temple is the home of big plump eels, overfed on offerings of boiled eggs which are conveniently sold by vendors at the gate. In another enclosure, the stones wound in white cloth with a yellow sash come from Gunung Rinjani, and Chinese Taoists have put mirrors there to repel the malevolent spirits.

At **Suranadi**, in the gardens just east of Lingsar, eggs are on the menu again, for the residents of a pond in the Temple of the Holy Eels. You can swim, too, in a separate spring-fed pool or at the old Dutch-built hotel, and even play golf at the nearby country club.

Monkeys wait by the roadside for handouts as you approach **Gunung Pensong**, a temple sited on top of a rocky outcrop 6 km (4 miles) south of the capital city, Mataram.

Senggigi Beach and the Gilis

Heading north along the coast from Ampenan, look out for
Pura Segara, a sea temple on the shore near a Chinese
cemetery. Close by, villagers gather to haul the fishing boats
up the beach and help sort the catch.

Batubolong temple stands perched on a rock—a good
lookout point to watch the sunset over the Lombok Strait.

The prime place to stay is around **Senggigi Beach**, just north
of Batubolong. There is accommodation in all sizes strung out
along a 10-km (6-mile) strip of coast starting about 8 km (5
miles) north of Ampenan. The beach shelves steeply in places
and the coral reef or rocks can be just below the surface, so it's
advisable to wear rubber shoes.

North of Senggigi, the road is one big giddy roller-coast-
er. At times it climbs to the cliff tops, and then swoops down
into bays. Tiny fishing villages hide among the palm trees
and the sea is flecked with bright lateen sails of *prahus* out
after tuna and snapper.

Instead of the coast road, tours from Senggigi and traffic from Mataram sometimes take the inland route via the
Pasuk Pass. The two ways meet at Pemenang, where a
side road leads to a harbour at **Bangsal**, the starting point
for trips to the Gilis. (Visitors often call them the Gili Islands, but *gili* means "island.") **Gili Air** is nearest, about
3 km (2 miles) away. Next comes **Gili Meno** and then
Gili Trawangan, the farthest out at 8 km (5 miles), and
the biggest, although it's only 2.5 km (1½ miles) long.

Snorkelling, diving, and sunning are the chief attractions
of the Gilis. The boats wait for a full load of 15 to 20 people.
In July and August that won't take long, but out of season
you can face a delay unless you pay for the empty places or
charter a whole boat (fares are low, and fixed).

*A hotel garden borders the beach at Senggigi ,
where beautiful coral lies right below the water's surface.*

There's *losmen* or bungalow accommodation on all three islands, as well as small stores where you can buy basic food, bottled water, and cold drinks. *Warungs* serve simple meals, mostly the standard Indonesian-style dishes and whatever fresh fish has come in.

Mountain Treks

The silhouette of Gunung Rinjani, 3,726 meters (12,200 feet) tall, can be seen from every part of the island, sometimes as a single peak, other times like a line of broken teeth.

An active volcano (although there has been no major eruption for a century), the mountain is sacred to both Sasaks and Balinese, who make pilgrimages to its crater lake and hot springs. Recently it has begun to attract foreigners, too, and two villages in the foothills to the south of Bayan are the most popular starting points. Trekking is only safe in the dry season, between June and September.

A rough and narrow road from the middle of Bayan ascends rapidly to **Batu Koq**, and then continues to nearby **Senaru**, where it ends. Those wanting to go farther have to walk. The original tiny village has traditional Sasak houses on stilts, surrounded by a wooden fence. Some of the locals have opened homestays along the road, a few with a *warung* attached. Guides and porters can be hired by the day, and you can buy basic food and rent camping gear, including tents. Take water purifying tablets, a small camping stove, and warm clothes.

The weavers of Sukarara at work producing their speciality, the gold- and silver-threaded songket fabric.

The main objective of most trekkers is the awesome crater with its big C-shaped lake. It's a hard day's walk from Senaru before you reach the rim. The crater itself is 600 meters (2,000 feet) deep, and the steep, quite slippery scramble down to the lake takes several hours more. Plan at least a three-day expedition (five if you also want to

The fragrant frangipani.

climb to the top of Rinjani). Those with a lot less time and energy could take a half-hour walk to a beautiful waterfall and pools in the valley below Senaru.

South and East Lombok

As in Bali, different areas specialize in particular crafts, but until recently it all happened behind closed doors. Now the increased tourist traffic has encouraged local people to set up stalls by the roadside, and some of the villages have become quite accustomed to visitors.

At **Sukarara**, to the south of Mataram, you will find almost every house has an old-fashioned loom for weaving the gorgeous *songket* fabric, which mingles gold and silver threads with cotton. **Penujak**, a little farther south, produces pottery, including some trick water pots which can be tipped upside down without spilling the contents. Invert them again and you can pour as normal. The secret of this manoeuvre is a clever interior partition.

Beleke, east of the market town of Praya, specializes in the craft of intricate basketry. They say that it takes them a week to make a large tablemat. **Rambitan** is a traditional type of Sasak village with thatch and bamboo houses and tall rice barns, but it sees a lot of visitors, and you may well be besieged by souvenir sellers. **Sade** is similar but smaller.

Farther south, the dry scrub-covered hills slowly give way to semi-desert, with an occasional grove of coconut palms playing the role of oasis. Energetic resurfacing and new construction has transformed the road, but **Kuta Beach** is still far from resembling its namesake in Bali. Most of the time, its white coral sands are largely deserted. Most accommodation is still in simple cottages, some with a modest restaurant as well: otherwise you can find a cheap *warung*. Just once a year in February or March, a few days after the second full moon of the year, crowds gather on the beach for Bau Nyale. The all-night festival is timed to coincide with the hatching of strange worms from the sea bed.

East of Narmada, near the main road that runs through Lombok, there is a cluster of craft villages. The baskets and tablemats from **Loyok** are famous throughout Indonesia. In neighbouring Rungkang, they make smooth jet-black pots of all sizes and then weave a fine basket to fit tightly around them, using supple lengths of ultra-thin rattan.

> In villages without official accommodation, make your presence known to the mayor. He can arrange for you to stay with a local family.

On the southern slopes of Gunung Rinjani, **Tete Batu** is a favourite local retreat, with an old hotel and a couple of homestays. Here you can walk to forest waterfalls, while the black monkeys chatter, squeal, and swing in the trees.

Labuhan Lombok is a hot, windswept, dusty, end-of-the-world sort of spot in spite of its picturesque stilt houses. The ferries laden with cars, motor bikes, and passengers sail several times a day to the east to the island of Sumbawa from a terminal 3 km (2 miles) from the village.

WHAT TO DO

SPORTS

The aim of most visitors to Bali or Lombok is to get in, on, or under the water as soon as possible. Almost every known method of watersport is on offer, and the range of land-based activities is growing, too. You can enjoy tennis and golf, hiking, and cycling, especially in the cool of the early morning (avoid the midday heat, at least until you have acclimatized). The more unusual spectator sports include colourful buffalo races, and the local favourite is cockfighting.

Watersports

Most resorts give you a choice of **swimming**. When the tide or sea conditions don't suit, there is usually the pool. If there isn't one where you are staying, you may be able to use another hotel's pool for a small charge. Some are set in elaborate gardens with slides and waterfalls: if they're too tame for you, you can make a bigger splash at Tuban's waterpark, south of Kuta.

Warm water, gorgeous coral, and vivid fish make for great **snorkelling** over the reefs, especially off the north coast of Bali, Nusa Lembongan, and Lombok's offshore Gilis (see page 77). Take your own equipment if you have it. Otherwise, many hotels will lend or rent it to you—check the fit and condition carefully. Superb sites for **scuba diving** include Menjangan and Nusa Penida off Bali, and the Gilis. Specialist tour operators rent out all the equipment and run courses for complete beginners— make sure that the company you choose is licensed and that the instructors are fully qualified, with international certification.

Plenty of Australians and, more recently, Japanese, come here only for the **surfing**. They head for the south and west coasts (Kuta, Uluwatu) in the dry season and the east side (Nusa Dua, Sanur) in

*You can enjoy sailing in a catamaran,
the descendant of the local outrigger jukung.*

the wet. In most places, local boys with outrigger boats are on hand
to transport them out beyond the reefs. Difficulty levels range from
middling to the extreme—there is no "nursery slope."

Jimbaran Bay has a **sailing** club, and you can **windsurf**
from most of the resort beaches: equipment can be rented at
Kuta, Benoa, Lovina, and Sanur. Conditions are not ideal for
beginners, though. Falling off on to coral is not only painful
—it can also harm the fragile ecosystem of the reef.

Whitewater rafting is one of the newer activities. Tour
companies will pick you up at your hotel, then take you to
the launch point on the Ayung river near Ubud, and provide
you with the necessary equipment for an exhilarating trip.

On Dry Land

The **golf** courses at Nusa Dua and up in the mountains at the
Bali Handara Kosaido Country Club are both top-class, staging tournaments which bring some of the world's best players. There's a 9-hole course at Sanur, and at Lombok there is
the 18-hole Suranadi course. Many hotels offer their own
tennis courts, some floodlit for evening use. Air-conditioned
squash courts are available at a few places. As the sun starts

to set, informal soccer and volleyball games between visitors and locals begin on the beach at Kuta, Tuban, and Legian.

If you choose to go **walking** in the countryside, don't start at the southern resorts, which are a long way from the best scenery, but begin instead up in the hills, where it's cooler.

More arduous and serious mountain **treks** include climbing the active volcano Gunung Batur—a trek of several hours—and the crater rim and lake of Gunung Rinjani (on Lombok), which demands at least three days to complete.

Spectator Sports

Regular **buffalo races** are held at Negara in western Bali, with the normally sluggish beasts pulling decorated carts at surprising speeds. **Kite flying** is a local obsession at Sanur and on the windswept Bukit Peninsula. Some of the huge constructions threaten to carry their owners aloft as well.

In Lombok, **ritual fights** long ago took the place of war. The Balinese and Sasaks hurl packets of cooked rice at each other in the October *perang ketupet* festival. Large crowds gather regularly in villages in Lombok to watch *peresehan* contests in which men armed with rattan canes and leather shields lash at each other until the referee declares one of them the victor.

ENTERTAINMENT

The sound of music in Bali can be the hypnotic tones of the *gamelan* orchestra, or the alluring call of the disco beat at Kuta or Legian, where the action begins at midnight and lasts until dawn. In the rest of the resorts the nightlife is on a much smaller scale.

Bali's own celebrated culture of dance and drama flourishes on two levels: for the visitors and for locals themselves. Ask at hotels, travel agencies, and tourist information offices to find out what is scheduled during your stay. They'll probably point you towards some of the commercial performances put on in several villages, mostly in the Ubud area. Tickets (including transport) are sold by the tourist office in Ubud and by many of the tour operators. Increasingly, the culture is packaged and brought to you in shows staged at hotels. Some of these are of a very high standard: dedicated dancers and musicians usually do give of their best. But inevitably the atmosphere is different when they are performing for un-tutored tourists eating dinner, rather than for an expert village audience—and above all for their gods.

Drama and dance students will think that they've gone to heaven when they see the unique temple ceremonies. If you are invited, be prepared to wait for a long time. Starting times are highly elastic, and then some events will last for many hours.

Many of the dances of Bali are also performed in western Lombok, either for the Balinese community there or, increasingly, for the tourists at Senggigi hotels. Lombok also has its own special dances, which are rarely staged commercially. Some are for men only: one simulating battle preparations probably derives from the Islamic tradition. The *gandrung* dance closely resembles Bali's *joged*, in that a girl picks a male partner from the audience. Another group of dances is based on romantic legends from Sasak mythology, dating back to before the advent of Islam. Western-

---

Take Care

The sea may look perfect for swimming, but it needs to be approached with caution. Rocks, coral, and sudden deep holes can lie concealed just below the water, especially at low tide. Sharp pieces of coral are a hazard almost every-where, so it's worth wearing rubber shoes whenever you enter the water. Waves breaking over reefs are especially dangerous: only swim or snorkel there in calm conditions. Take local advice, only swim between marker flags, don't swim or surf alone, and acknowledge your limitations.

Gamelan intrumentalists producing the unmistakable traditional music of Bali.

style nightlife is limited to Senggigi, where some hotels run discos and local groups play in the bar-restaurants.

The puppet shadow plays called *wayang kulit* (leather puppet) are not so often put on for tourists—the plots are too complex and the shows last too long for foreign consumption. A temple ceremony may give you a chance to join the audience for a while, and then look behind the screen—it's permitted—to see the *dalang* or puppet master expertly controlling the beautiful figures, speaking all their lines in a vast range of appropriate voices and conducting the small orchestra.

Dances of Bali

Legong: This is the visitors' favourite dance, performed by three young girls: two principal dancers, the legongs, no more than 12 or 13 years old, and an attendant. Each is exquisitely dressed in glittering songket fabrics and wears a gilded and jewelled headdress embellished with fresh frangipani (plumeria) flowers. The usual version (*legong kraton*) is the tale of a king and the princess he has abducted, performed by the two principals who, using various hand and facial gestures, portray the attempted seduction

Kecak: Part of a much longer ritual trance-dance which is called *sanghyang*, this is mostly performed separately. Up to 150 men in sarongs crouch in concentric circles round a flickering lamp. They sit up uttering sharp cries, then slump down with a hiss and staccato chattering, followed by deep rhythmic chanting. Suddenly they fall back together. The story acted out in the centre of the circle, taken from the Ramayana, concerns Rama and Sita and the monkey armies of Hanuman and Sugriwa, hence the *kecak's* popular title of "Monkey Dance."

Pendet: Six or more girls carrying trays of flower petals open the evening by scattering the petals over the stage as a symbol of welcome. At the same time, a man may light an incense-burning lamp. At temple ceremonies the *pendet* is danced to welcome the gods.

Janger: Twelve boys and twelve girls in groups of six form a square, the girls kneeling and swaying together to the music like reeds in the wind. The boys, wearing false moustaches, try to impress the girls as they strut and preen like fighting cocks.

Joged: A whole family of dances shares this name, performed to the music of an orchestra of bamboo xylophones and gongs. But one, properly called the *jegog*, has become so popular that it alone is often considered to be *joged*. A young woman

---

Gamelan

Impossible to describe, unmistakable once you have heard it, the bell-like sound of a *gamelan* orchestra is Bali's musical heartbeat. You'll hear the players practising when you stroll through a village, or see them in their matching shirts and sarongs, loading their instruments onto the back of a truck to set off for an engagement somewhere. A gamelan orchestra will accompany most of the dance performances at the hotels as well as at every temple festival. There must be tens of thousands of such groups, all different. Each banjar has at least one, with its own unique collection of valuable instruments — gongs, metallophones (metal versions of xylophones), drums, cymbals, and flutes. They are tuned to two different five-note "scales" instead of the Western octave.

Gamelan came to Bali from Java and still flourishes there, but after four centuries of separation it has evolved differently and taken on its own character.

The Ramayana epic is told in ballet form.

dances alone at first, and then taps members of the audience in turn to dance with her. Try as they may to flirt or show off, she easily slips away from their advances. Few Westerners look anything but clumsy in comparison.

Barong: A mythical lion-like animal, the *barong* is covered in long hair and little mirrors. Animated by two men, it fights against the evil Rangda, queen of the witches. Her long claw-like fingernails hold a white cloth to hide her terrible face, bulging eyes, fangs, and flaming tongue while she advances on her victims. Allies of the barong, men wearing sarongs and each carrying a *kris*, try to attack Rangda but she puts them under a spell. In a trance, they turn the knives on themselves. Only the reappearance of the barong saves them.

In daily performances for visitors (each morning at Batubulan, for instance) the trances are inevitably simulated. Late at night in a village, however, you would see the wild-eyed men in a genuine frenzy or collapsing at the climax into unconsciousness, until revived by priests who sprinkle them with holy water.

Other Dances: Other performances you might see include scenes from the Hindu epic drama, the Ramayana, staged as a ballet. These may well be a showcase for fine dancing, gorgeous costumes, and the full range of the gamelan orchestra. In the *topeng*, the dancers are masked, meaning that they can convey character and emotion through movement alone. The stories are taken from Balinese history and mythology.

Kebyar is the name of a group of solo dances of which the best known are performed by a seated man, using only the upper body. *Baris* is a vehicle for groups of young male dancers to display their command of technique, conveying a great range of emotions.

FESTIVALS AND EVENTS

Most festivals are fixed by calendars different from the Western version (see box page 91), so they change each year. Look out for the Indonesian Directorate of Tourism's annual *Calendar of Events*, which is published in Bali and gives dates and locations of temple festivals. Two celebrations stick to fixed dates: The **Walter Spies** festival in February and the summer **Arts Festival** in June and July.

SHOPPING

Bali produces a wide range and large quantity of craftwork in every medium. Most of the decorative arts and crafts originally had a religious connection, as temple embellishment, offerings, or ceremonial dress. The land yielded plenty to eat without the need to work all day, every day, so people had time to create objects of beauty. The tradition continues, although production has been multiplied by the demand for souvenirs. Some craft shops in the villages have workshops attached, or you can watch the carvers, painters, or weavers in the adjoining compound.

The Ramayana epic is also told in shadow plays using puppets.

In the past, nothing was expected to last: the climate and insects saw to that. So hardly anything is very old—"Antiques Made to Order" shop signs give the game away.

Wood carvings: Dozens of villages devote themselves to Bali's biggest craft business; Mas (see page 42) is the best-known, with hundreds of carvers and countless shops. Behind the scenes—but you may be invited for a visit—fathers pass on their skills to their sons, while the women do the polishing or painting. The best carvings are superb sculptures, but even the simplest, cheapest article can make an appealing souvenir. Among the massed garuda birds and masks, you're bound to find something beautiful.

The sign "Parasite Carvings" might puzzle you. A new idea, imported from the West, is to take the galls and other strange growths that occur on tree trunks and carve them into a witty or grotesque design, using the natural shape.

Carvings of mythical birds make appealing souvenirs.

Jewellery: The village of Celuk (see page 41) had specialized in producing silver and gold jewellery for centuries, so when tourism arrived, its position on the Denpasar-Ubud road was ideal. Dozens of tour buses stop at the big shops but there are several little workshops worth visiting, too. The smiths can produce any style: from intiricate filigree work to simple bracelets. You don't have to go to Celuk though, since every resort area has its share of shops. Silver should bear the "925" stamp of sterling silver (meaning it's 92.5% pure).

Useful abbreviations:
- PPN (Pajak Pertambahan Nilai)—sales tax, VAT
- Jl. (Jalan)—street, road
- Gg (Gang)—lane
- p.p. (pulang pergi)—return/roundtrip

Clothes and Fabrics: Bali is a huge bargain basement for a selection of beachwear, casual clothing, and, at a higher price but still excellent value, fashion designs. For the biggest choice of shops go to Kuta, and look for dresses, shirts, sarongs, and cover-ups in traditional *batik* fabric.

The batik dyeing technique uses hot wax to draw or stamp a design on cloth before dipping it in the dye, so that the waxed areas are left undyed. The process can be repeated a number of times for greater complexity. Java is the source of the batik for dresses and sarongs sold in fashion shops; Balinese versions are usually much coarser. Hawkers will swear that their dress lengths of cheap printed cotton are batik,

---

Days and Dates

The Balinese *puwukon* calendar consists of 30 weeks (*wuku*) of seven days each. Confusingly superimposed on that are other "weeks," which can be anything from one to ten days. Every 210 days comes the great national holiday of the god **Galungan**, a 10-day festival for the supreme god, always beginning on a Wednesday. Tall bamboo poles bearing bright flowers and palm leaf decorations stand at the gate of each house. Ancestral spirits are believed to visit the home of their forefathers, where they are lavishly entertained. On the 11th day, **Kuningan**, farewell offerings of yellow rice are set out for them.

If you can't afford a genuine batik, the printed imitations make a striking substitute.

pointing to the wording on the selvedge. It's easy to tell that they are not: printed patterns don't penetrate fully to the other side, while the real batik will show thin veins of colour where the dye runs along tiny cracks in the wax (printed versions may try to simulate this); and real batik is *much* more expensive.

Endek or *ikat* fabrics, using threads dyed in patterns before weaving, come from Gianyar in Bali as well as other Indonesian islands. In Bali, only the weavers of Tenganan make *grinsing*, or double *ikat*, using pattern-dyed threads for both warp and weft. The genuine fabric is justifiably expensive — beware of fakes!

Don't accept worn *rupiah* bills. You may have difficulty passing them on.

Paintings: If you want a unique work of art, you'll need to study the field. Visit the major collections to judge the standard of the best paintings, especially the Neka Museum and Museum Puri Lukisan in Ubud (see pages 42-43) as well as the Arts Centre in Denpasar (see page 39). Don't just assume that a high price guarantees original work.

And More... Look out for the **basketry** from Bona, leather *wayang kulit* **puppets** from Puaya near Sukawati, and decorative **umbrellas** on roadside stalls east of Klungkung.

Shops take advantage of the tourist traffic to sell the products of other islands, too—**embroidery** and *songket* **fabrics** from Sumatra, **primitive art** from Irian Jaya, and **silver** from Sulawesi.

Lombok: Craft skills in Lombok tend to be devoted to household objects that can have a somewhat austere functional beauty. Look out for the delicate, tightly-woven basketware, whether in mats, boxes, bowls, and bags, or the common Lombok souvenir of a model rice-barn. Painted wood boxes to store spices, tobacco, or jewellery are attractive. Simple red pottery comes from Penujak, and black pots from Rungkang are bound in an intricately woven basket.

Necessities: Some supermarkets and convenience stores have opened in Denpasar, such as Tiara Dewata, on Jalan

---

Bargaining

Love it or loathe it, there's no escape unless you go to a modern fixed-price store or supermarket. Otherwise, practically every purchase, large or trivial, will be the subject of a session of haggling. Here are a few suggestions:

- If possible, have some idea of the going rate before you start. Identical items may be offered for Rp1,000 in one place and Rp25,000 in another. Hotel shops tend to be the most expensive, but the best of them have genuine treasures you won't find anywhere else.

- You will do better if you are not part of a group.

- Make the seller name a price first.

- If you automatically offer half that figure —the beginner's usual mistake—you've already lost the contest. The seller might have accepted one-fifth, or less, but now you will never know.

Jenderal Sutoyo, with books, shoes, cosmetics, and even a playground for children and swimming pool. There is a similar big shopping centre near the airport, while smaller ones can be found in Kuta, Nusa Dua, Senggigi, and Lombok.

> The plural meaning is sometimes conveyed by doubling the noun: *anak-anak* (**children**), *kue-kue* (**deserts**).

CHILDREN'S BALI

The Balinese treasure their children and yours will get the

same treatment. Some resorts run children's activity programmes during the day, show videos in the early evening, and at night offer a babysitting service when you want to go off on your own. In *losmen* and home-stay accommodation, the children of the owning family will probably want to make friends, and the older girls may offer to act as babysitters.

Children's programmes are organized by many of the hotels to give the parents a break.

Children will, of course, revel in the hotel pools and the beaches, the slides at the Waterbom park in Tuban, and when the conditions are right, they can learn to snorkel, sail, and windsurf —but think about their safety.

EATING OUT

The countless places to eat in Bali fall into three broad categories: the hotels, the restaurants aimed at foreign visitors, and those intended mainly for the Balinese. Each type is certainly worth trying.

The choice in Lombok is far more limited. There's a lack of notable restaurants either in or outside the hotels. The word *lombok* actually means a red chilli pepper: so watch out for it in the local dishes.

Where to Eat

You will find that hotels usually have at least one restaurant. In the big resorts, there may be a whole range, offering Japanese, Chinese, or Thai food, and "international" and Indonesian, too. Some places can be dull, and some are excellent by any standard, with prices to match.

Many hotels regularly stage themed buffet nights: seafood, a barbecue, or a *Pasar Malam* (Night Market), where interesting foodstalls entice you with dishes from all round the Pacific, or from every Southeast Asian nation. A good *rijsttafel* (Dutch for rice table), comprising a banquet of side dishes accompanying rice, is a fine way to experience a range of cooking in the Indonesian tradition. Compare the prices of these hotel events — often they include entertainment and can be excellent value and are also a good way to sample a variety of different styles of cooking.

Most eating places in Indonesia used to be Chinese-run (many still are today), and the food is a hybrid of Chinese and Malay. *Nasi goreng*, which consists of fried rice, lightly spiced with chillies and garlic and combined with some finely chopped vegetables and a little meat, chicken, or a few shrimps—menus usually list the options—is practically the national dish. *Nasi rames* is white rice with vegetable and meat dishes; *ba kmi goreng* means similar combinations but based on rice-flour noodles. In *nasi campur* the rice is boiled and then topped with the same sorts of extras as *nasi goreng*. Instead of bread you'll get *krupuk*, large prawn crackers, which accompany most Indonesian meals.

> *Rijsttafel* is not an authentic Indonesian dish but was invented by the Dutch.

Spices and flavours may be toned down to the tastes of foreigners. Ask for dishes to be *pedas* (spicy) if that is what you want. Some places respond by bringing you a bottle of *sambal*, ultra-hot chilli, lime, and prawn paste.

Local cooking is colourful and often spicy.

If you want a cheaper meal you can choose between one of the corner stalls (*warung*), a dining room (*rumah makan*), or a more modest restaurant serving standard Indonesian fare. These cater mostly for locals but you will be very welcome.

What to Eat

When tourist numbers began to build up, so did the demand for alternatives to the typical Indonesian diet, starting with the Australians, who called for "good Aussie tucker" (still to be found in Kuta). Although fashions and fads came and went, Italian, Indian, and Mexican restaurants have proved to be durable.

The "seafood market" concept has arrived in Bali—you make your choice from a big display and hand it over to be cooked. Giant prawns and lobster come top of the price list, charged per 100 grams, so keep an eye on the cost or the bill can be quite a shock. Little restaurants near the fishing beaches may have fresh tuna, barracuda, whole snapper, and shark steaks. They're delicious when lightly grilled but too often are fried in poor-quality oil.

Tasty mini kebabs, called sate, are a tasty Balinese treat.

Hindus are not supposed to eat beef, but most of the animals that look like cows are water buffalo, and some Balinese will eat their meat. There is no apparent reluctance to serve beef to others, so you can order a pretty good steak, perhaps imported from New Zealand or Australia.

Bali has its own convenience foods, too: *pisang goreng*, crispy fried banana slices, and *sate* (or *satay*)— mini-kebabs of tender meat, prawns, or fish cooked over charcoal and served with a squeeze of lime juice and

peanut sauce. The crunchy fried dragonflies find fewer foreign takers.

Balinese Dishes

Bali's specialities are mainly reserved for festivals. Simplified versions turn up on a few restaurant menus, and big hotel kitchens sometimes show off their skills by including Balinese dishes in their buffet events.

At all the big temple ceremonies or family celebrations you will find *lawar*, in which cooked and finely chopped meat and offal of a pig or turtle, steamed vegetables, grated coconut, plenty of garlic, shallots, hot red chillies, and fresh spices are subtly combined by an expert. Raw minced meat, blood, and lime juice are mixed in before serving the colourful *lawar* on a banana leaf. A *lawar* on a hotel buffet usually omits the raw meat and blood.

The local ducks may appear on the table, in the form of *bebek betutu*, in which they are rubbed and stuffed with a fiery mixture of chillies, garlic, and spices. Or, a whole duck is wrapped in layers of banana leaves before being cooked slowly in a clay oven. Thus it is steamed, roasted, and smoked simultaneously, and the meat should practically fall off the bones. Restaurant versions can be disappointing.

> Any dish with *padang* in its name is likely to be hot.

In the rest of Indonesia, most people are Muslims and don't eat pork. In Bali, the reverse applies: to Hindus, pork is permitted. *Babi guling*, spit-roasted young pig — suckling pig is a rare luxury — is the centrepiece of many a banquet. Once stuffed with finely-chopped chillies, garlic, ginger, and spices, the pig is roasted until it's cooked through and the skin is crisp.

When dining with Balinese, help yourself generously to rice, then take just a little from side dishes. Wait to be asked by your host to start eating or drinking. The left hand is considered unclean, so when passing food or eating with your fingers use the right hand.

Desserts

Your best bets are the fresh fruit: mangoes, bananas, passionfruit, mandarin oranges, and the less familiar rambutan (small, red, and hairy), rose apple, custard apple, and *salak* (or snakefruit), covered in hard brown scales. Black rice pudding is just that—boiled black rice served with sweetened coconut milk. Pancakes have caught on here—try them with fresh pineapple and banana.

Drinks

Oranges, bananas, pineapples, and some tropical fruits are pulped into delicious juices, but make sure you are buying from a hygienic source. You will find bottled water and bottled drinks sold

> It is considered good manners not to drain your glass but to leave a little at the bottom.

everywhere in Bali, even at the smallest foodstall. A pot of not-too-strong tea without milk makes a good accompaniment to a typical Indonesian meal. So, too, does the good local beer.

The best Balinese rice wine, *brem*, is something like Japanese sake, but most of it is usually too sweet and oxidized; it's the base of a lot of fruit cocktails. Imported drinks are expensive and wine costs a lot more than it would in Australia—which is where most of it comes from.

To Help You Order...

To help you get the most out of eating in Bali, we recommend the Berlitz *Indonesian Phrase Book and Dictionary*, which has a comprehensive section covering eating out.

I would like ...		Saya ingin ...	
beer	**bir**	milk	**susu**
bread	**roti**	orange juice	**air jeruk**
breakfast	**makan pagi**	pepper	**merica**
butter	**mentega**	salt	**garam**
coffee	**kopi**	sugar	**gula**
dinner	**makan malam**	tea	**teh**
fruit	**buah-buahan**	the menu	**daftar makanan**
ice cream	**es krim**	water	**air**
lunch	**makan siang**	wine	**anggur**

... and Read the Menu

asam manis	sweet and sour	**kecap**	soy sauce
ayam	chicken	**kelapa**	coconut
babi	pork	**kentang**	potato
babi guling	spit-roast pork	**kepiting**	crab
ba kmi	noodles	**krupuk**	prawn-flavoured rice crackers
bebek betutu	roast smoked duck		
bistik	steak	**mangga**	mango
bubur	rice porridge	**manggis**	mangosteen
capcai	stir-fried vegetables	**markisa**	passion-fruit
		mie	noodles
domba	lamb	**nanas**	pineappple
gado gado	vegetables and peanut sauce	**nasi putih**	plain rice (steamed)
goreng	fried	**soto**	soup
ikan	fish	**telur**	egg
jambu biji	guava	**udang**	lobster
kare	curry (mild)	**karang**	

INDEX

Where there is more than one set of references, the one in **bold** refers to the main entry. References in *italics* refer to an illustration.

HANDY TRAVEL TIPS

An A–Z Summary of Practical Information

A

ACCOMMODATION (See also CAMPING on page 107, YOUTH HOSTELS on page 128 , and the list of RECOMMENDED HOTELS starting on page 130)

The range of **hotels** and other places to stay in Bali should suit every taste and budget. There's a handful of exclusive luxury retreats, and a few top international hotels in a similar high-price bracket. Somewhat less expensive are the many places designed mainly for the package tour business and concentrated in the resort areas. In many hotels, the accommodation is in separate cottages or villas, often using traditional local materials and architecture.

A **losmen** is a small, family-run hotel. The word **homestay** was coined some years ago to convey the idea of living with a local family on a room-and-breakfast or room-and-board basis. Nowadays the terms *losmen* and homestay are used interchangeably. They can be anything from a small beach resort to a traditional family compound with a room to let, or even a plain commercial hotel. You really need to see the accomodation to know whether or not it will suit you. The owners are quite used to showing rooms to prospective clients, and to a certain amount of bargaining over the price.

Rates quoted are generally for room only, although the more modest places often include a basic breakfast. There is only a small difference (or none) between rates for single or double occupancy.

All hotels add tax of 10% and a service charge of 10% to the bill, compounded to 21%. This may not be included in the quoted rates.

Lombok has far fewer visitors than Bali, most of whom stay in the holiday hotels along the coastal strip around Senggigi. There are business-oriented hotels and homestays in the Ampenan-Mataram-Cakranegara urban area and scattered round the island in towns and the small number of tourist targets, particularly the Gili Islands.

Do you have any vacancies?   **Apakah masih ada kamar yang kosong?**

a single/double room   **kamar untuk satu/dua orang**

with bath/shower	**dengan kamar mandi atau/shower**

AIRPORTS

Ngurah Rai Airport, **Denpasar** (Code DPS), at the southern end of the island, is 10 km (6 miles) from Denpasar.

Telephone number: (0361) 25662.

Some hotels operate shuttle buses, and other minibus services run to and from all parts of Bali. Taxis are arranged by a central desk where you exit the terminal. Prices are fixed and payable in advance.

The airport has a 24-hour exchange office and duty-free shops.

A departure tax is charged, payable in cash after check-in for international flights. Ask at your hotel for the latest information, as the amount of the tax changes frequently. The lower rate for domestic flights is usually included in the ticket price.

Selaparang Airport, **Lombok** (code AMI), is 1.5 km (1 mile) from Mataram and about 12 km (7 miles) from the resort area of Senggigi.

B

BICYCLE and MOTORCYCLE HIRE

In spite of the heat and erratic drivers, two wheels are not a bad way to get around. In fact they are the local favourite means of travel. Plenty of **bicycles** are available to rent (hire). Your hotel may recommend a place or even have bicycles of its own. Insist on a modern mountain bike (Indonesia is a major manufacturer). You will appreciate its low gears on the steep hills and its shock-absorbing tires: the minor roads and paths are often rough. Check the condition of wheels, spokes, tires, and brakes. Front and back brakes should function well, and using either should be able to bring you to a stop. You'll need a bell that works and, ideally, reflectors (although riding at night is not advised). In case of a puncture or breakdown, wheel your bike to the repair shop that you'll find in almost every village.

Don't consider renting a **motorcycle** unless you are already an experienced rider. The unpredictable habits of other road users, including sundry livestock, and the rough surfaces and potholes will call for skilful handling. You need your licence as well as an international licence, valid for motorcycles. Some of the machines for rent may be the private property of one person, and the agreement may be very informal, with doubtful insurance coverage. You might have to hand over your passport as a deposit, as well as pay in advance. If you are not happy with this, look for a larger agency. Always check the condition of the machine carefully before accepting it.

C

CAMPING *(berkemah)*

With plenty of economical alternatives available, few people bother to camp. Rain, mosquitoes, and especially the lack of security make camping a less attractive option anyway. Only on longer mountain treks in Lombok will you actually need to camp, and the equipment can be rented locally.

CAR HIRE *(sewa mobil)* (See also DRIVING on page 112)

Self-drive car rental (hirc) is easily arranged through one of the many local companies. In fact, a lot of signs offering rental vehicles arc put up by agencies who merely pass you on to another company—and collect a commission. To rent a self-drive vehicle, you should have a licence from your own country and an International Driving Licence, although you may not be asked to show them. The minimum age is usually 25, sometimes 21. Payment in advance for the whole of the rental period is usually expected. Some companies accept major credit cards. Always bargain for discounts. You will probably be able to negotiate a lower price for longer rental periods, or if demand is slack. Compare several different operators if you have the time.

A Jeep-type vehicle with high ground clearance is essential if you intend to get off the busy main roads. The most common vehicle on offer is the locally-assembled Suzuki. This is sturdy enough but has almost no luggage space. Open vehicles may sound like a good idea, but they make it difficult to safeguard your possessions, and also let in the rain and dust.

Bali

The condition of rental cars varies greatly, so take a test drive before accepting the vehicle. Make sure that all previous damage is recorded.

Insurance can present problems. The better companies have agreements with big insurers and will issue a policy document. Others are more casual, assuring you that insurance is "included." Try to get written evidence of just what is covered. Check all wording carefully before signing the rental agreement.

If rental difficulties and driving conditions (see DRIVING below) should put you off, you can spend about 75% more and rent a **car with a driver**. This has the great advantage that the driver will be responsible for the vehicle, dealing with problems and perhaps acting as a guide and interpreter.

CLIMATE and CLOTHING *(pakaian)*

This close to the equator (at a latitude of just 80 south), temperatures remain fairly stable year round. In lowland areas, they range from a nightly minimum of 24°C (75°F) to an average daily high of 30°C (86°F) in the shade. Mountain areas can be a lot cooler. The rainy season runs from December to March, although most days will see some sunshine. It's dry from June to September, and intermediate months are changeable. Humidity is high at all times of the year.

Clothing. The best advice is to travel light. You will rarely need anything more than summer clothes, preferably loose-fitting cottons, and Bali is a good place to buy casual and beach wear inexpensively. The local sarong can be a useful accessory for men as well as women. Brief or revealing dress is only acceptable in the resort areas. On visits to religious sites, you'll need to cover up. Anyone wearing shorts, a tank top, or bikini top will give offence and probably won't be allowed in, although at many temples you can solve the problem by renting a sarong. It's also advisable to dress respectably when visiting government and other offices. Long sleeves and a hat are recommended whenever you are likely to be out in the sun for any length of time. Out of doors in the evenings, protect arms and legs against mosquitoes. It can be considerably cooler in the hills, and if you plan an expedition to the mountains prepare for it to be positively chilly at night.

Indonesians are quite fashion-conscious, and many visitors in the resort hotels also like to dress up in the evening. A long-sleeved batik or white shirt is standard semi-formal wear for men.

Remember to take the following as it might be difficult, and a waste of time, trying to find them locally: Sun protection and sunblock; sunglasses and sun hat; earplugs (dogs bark all night in the villages and cocks crow long before dawn); rubber shoes for swimming near reefs—coral fragments are sharp and so are sea-urchin spines; mosquito repellent.

COMMUNICATIONS (See also TIME DIFFERENCES on page 125) **Post offices** (*pos kantor*). They are usually jammed with people, and Denpasar's is some way from the centre in Jalan Raya Puputan, Renon. It's more convenient to buy stamps at postal agencies (*agen pos*) run by many small shops, or at the larger hotels, even if you are not staying there. Important mail should be registered.

If you don't know ahead of time where you will be staying, you may have mail addressed to you c/o Poste Restante, Pos Kantor at Kuta, Sanur, Ubud, or one of the bigger towns.

airmail/registered	**pos udara/pos tercatat**
A stamp for this letter/postcard, please.	**Saya perlu perangko untuk surat/kartupos ini.**

Telephone (*telepon*). Direct dialling has now been introduced in most of Bali. The area code for southern Bali is 0361; for Lombok 0370. The code for Indonesia from other countries is 62, followed by the area code (omitting the initial 0) and then the number required.

For international calls *from* Indonesia, dial 001, then the country code, area code (omitting initial 0) and local number. For an international operator, dial 102.

Hotels add extra charges, sometimes large ones, to telephone calls. You may do better by using one of the calling cards issued by international telephone companies (hotels then charge only for a local call).

At the highly efficient WARTEL offices, found in most towns and resort areas, you can make local and international calls, both economically and without delay. You can see the amount you are spending on a visual display and the bill is printed out as soon as you end the call. Some shops also offer the same service but charge more.

Faxes. The larger hotels will send and receive faxes for you. So will some WARTEL agencies and business offices.

COMPLAINTS *(pengaduan)*
If you have a problem with a hotel, restaurant, or shop, ask to see the manager and explain the difficulty; avoid becoming enmeshed in bureaucracy — which can waste a lot of time.

CRIME (See also Emergencies on page 113 and Police on page 124)
Take commonsense precautions and be on your guard. Put valuables in your hotel safe and don't leave any desirable items unguarded while you go for a swim. Watch out for pickpockets, especially in crowded places and on *bemos* and other public transport.

Muggings are almost unheard of, but there have been cases of bag-snatching. Don't wear expensive-looking jewellery and carry only the cash you need. If you do have something of value stolen, you will need to report the loss to a police station to obtain a document to show your insurance company.

The possession, sale, import, and export of narcotic drugs is illegal and punished by severe jail sentences and fines. Anyone offering you drugs is quite likely to be an informer.

My ticket/wallet/passport has been stolen.	**Ticket/dompet/passpor saya telah dicuri orang.**

CUSTOMS *(pabean)* and ENTRY FORMALITIES
To enter Indonesia as a tourist, you need a passport valid for at least six months from the date of entry. Visitors from Australia, New

Zealand, Canada, the U.K., U.S.A., Japan, and many other countries do not need a visa. You may be asked to show an onward or return ticket or evidence of funds for its purchase. The length of stay is limited to 60 days. Business visitors may need a visa; travel agents or Indonesian embassies can tell you how to obtain one.

If you are carrying any medication that might be mistaken for an illegal drug, bring a letter from your doctor or copy of a prescription. Weapons and ammunition are forbidden. So are publications in Chinese. Larger and expensive items should be registered in your passport. If you have nothing to declare, you can use the green lane.

No more than Rp50,000 in local currency may be brought into or taken out of the country. There is no restriction on foreign currency.

Duty-free. When entering Indonesia (two-week stay) travellers may carry the following: 2 litres of alcoholic drinks (opened bottles); 100 cigars **or** 400 cigarettes **or** 200 grams tobacco; gifts of a total value up to US$100. Restrictions when returning to your own country are as follows:

Into:	Cigarettes		Cigars		Tobacco	Spirits		Wine
Malta	200 or 250 g of other tobacco products*					1 l	or	1 l
Australia	200	or	250 g	or	250 g	1 l	and	1 l
Canada	200	or	50	or	900 g	1.1 l	or	1.1 l
Eire	200	and	50	or	250 g	1 l	and	2 l
N. Zealand	200	or	50	or	250 g	1.1 l	and	4.5 l
S. Africa	400	and	50	and	250 g	1 l	and	2 l
UK	200	or	50	or	250 g	1 l	and	2 l
USA	200	and	100	and	**	1 l	or	1 l

* of which not more than 50 g in loose tobacco
** a reasonable quantity

D

DRIVING *(mengendarai)* (See also CAR HIRE on page 107)

In the southern part of Bali, roads are often choked with motorbikes, *bemos*, trucks, bicycles, wandering pedestrians, and animals. The towns are an inferno of noise and fumes, and the rest of the main road network can often seem like one continuous village street. Elsewhere, especially north of Klungkung or Mengwi, there's much less traffic and driving becomes a pleasure.

Nominally, traffic keeps to the left. It is legal to turn left, with care, at a red light.

Most major roads are well-surfaced, but in remoter regions they can be rough and tortuous. Direction signs are reasonably good. Always carry your driver's licence.

Fuel and oil. Petrol (gasoline) is available in the grade needed by most rental vehicles: pumps are marked "Premium." Filling stations are confined to the main towns, but most villages have a dealer with drums of fuel who will measure out the amount you want. The price is slightly more. Look for the sign "Premium" (sometimes "Permium") or, on Lombok, a red drum and funnel. Diesel is also obtainable: pumps are marked SOLAR.

Fluid measures

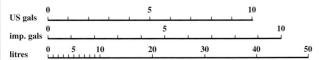

Distance

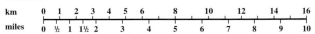

International Driving Permit	**Surat Ijin Mengemudi (SIM) Internasional**
Car registration papers	**Surat-surat kendaraan**
Where's the nearest service station?	**Dimanakah pompa bensin terdekat?**
Full tank, please.	**Fulteng/tolong diisi penuh.**
Check the oil/tyres/battery, please?	**Tolong periksa olinya/ban/aki.**
My car has broken down.	**Mobil saya rusak.**

E

ELECTRICITY *(listrik)*
Most hotels are on 220-volt, 50-cycle supply, and use plugs with two rounded pins. A few areas are on 110 volts. Bathroom shaver outlets often have both. Larger hotels may have transformers and adaptors.

EMBASSIES *(kedutaan besar)* **and CONSULATES**
Australia is the only English-speaking country to have a fully-fledged consulate in Bali, at: Jalan M. Yamin, Kav. 51, Renon, Denpasar; tel. (0361) 235092.

There's a U.S. consular agent at Jalan Hayam Wuruk 188, Denpasar; tel. (0361) 233605. Otherwise, representation is usually through the embassies in Jakarta.

Canada: 5th Floor, Wisma Metropolitan 1, Jalan Jen. Sudirman, Kav. 29, PO Box 8324, Jakarta; tel. (021) 5250709.

New Zealand: Jalan Diponegoro 41, Jakarta; tel. (021) 330680.

Singapore: Jalan H.R. Rasuna Said, Kav. 2, Blok X/4, Jakarta; tel. (021) 5201489.

U.K.: Jalan M.H. Thamrin 75, Jakarta; tel. (021) 330904.

U.S.A.: Jalan Merdeka Selatan 5, Jakarta; tel. (021) 3442211.

EMERGENCIES *(darurat)* (See also MEDICAL CARE on page 119 and POLICE on page 124)
The following telephone numbers may be useful:

police	**110**
fire brigade	**113**
ambulance	**118**

ENVIRONMENTAL ISSUES

You may be tempted to buy exotic souvenirs for you and your family on your holiday, but spare a thought for endangered plants and animals that may be threatened by your purchase. Even trade in tourist souvenirs can threaten the most endangered species.

Over 800 species of animals and plants are currently banned from international trade by CITES (Convention on International Trade in Endangered Species and Plants). These include many corals, shells, cacti, orchids, and hardwoods, as well as the more obvious tigers, rhinos, spotted cats, and turtles.

So think twice before you buy—it may be illegal and your souvenirs could be confiscated by Customs on your return.

For further information or a factsheet, contact the following:

U.K.—Department of the Environment; tel. 01179 878961 (birds, reptiles, and fish), or 01179 878168 (plants and mammals).

U.S.—Fish and Wildlife Service; tel. (703) 358-2095; fax (001) (703) 358-2281.

ETIQUETTE (See also RELIGION on page 124)

Except for a few who have learned bad habits from foreigners, Indonesians are instinctively courteous, gentle, and respectful to older people. They don't like to give negative or disappointing answers to questions. If you ask when or if some event is going to happen, you'll probably receive an encouraging response, even from someone who knows nothing at all about it.

It is polite to shake hands on meeting and taking your leave. Only your right hand is used for passing food or gifts, and for eating. When eating with local people, don't start until invited to do so by the host. Beef should not be offered to Hindus, although some consider water buffalo to be permissible. Pork and some shellfish are forbidden to Muslims.

Pointing at someone with a finger, beckoning, and standing with hands on hips or in your pockets are all seen as rude, aggressive gestures. Indicating an object with your foot—an item for sale in a street market for example—is worse still. Showing the sole of your shoe or foot is also insulting. Never touch anyone (not even little children) on the head.

Your legs and preferably arms as well should be covered when you enter a Hindu temple, and it is polite (and often required) to wear a sash. Take off your shoes before entering a mosque. Loud talking is considered to be inappropriate in a temple or mosque.

As you walk about, children and others will shout "Hello" and ask: *"Dari mana?"* ("Where are you from?") You can spend all day answering them, but "Hello" and a smile is a friendly enough response.

G

GAY and LESBIAN TRAVELLERS
Family influence is so strong that local people are all expected to get married eventually. Meanwhile, private liaisons—if they're discreet —are one's own affair. The same attitude applies to the sexual orientation of visitors. Public displays of affection are frowned on (especially in Lombok).

GUIDES *(pengantar)* and TOURS
If you are on an organized tour, guides will be provided. Otherwise, you can hire one on the spot when you visit major sites of interest. There may indeed be too many volunteers for the job, some knowledgeable and multilingual, others merely a nuisance. Hiring one has the merit of keeping the rest at bay.

Many hotels have tour desks offering a range of excursions, near and far. It's worth comparing prices with those charged by local agencies, and also to find out which tours are most enjoyable. One way is to ask other guests who have been on them.

L

LANGUAGE *(bahasa)*

The national language is Bahasa Indonesia (or just "Bahasa"), understood by most people although among themselves the Balinese speak their own complex language. It is not difficult to learn a few words and phrases of Bahasa Indonesia, and well worth the effort so that you can be polite and even ask a few simple questions. Everyone will respond cheerfully if you try.

Vowels are pronounced:

a like ah, but shorter **u** as in food
e as in met **ai** as in like
i usually as in meet; **au** as in cow
otherwise as in sit
o as in soft

Consonants generally are pronounced as in English, except:

c as in chin **k** at the end of a word is almost silent
g as in guest **r** is well-rolled

A slight emphasis is often placed on the last syllable of a word.

In addition to the words listed below, we would recommend the Berlitz *Indonesian Phrase Book and Dictionary*.

banjar	local community (area or council)
bapak	father, term of polite address to older man
bemo	minibus operating as a shared taxi
bukit	hill
desa	village
dokar	pony cart
gamelan	Balinese orchestra of gongs and xylophones
gang	alleyway, path
gili	island
gunung	mountain
homestay	bed & breakfast, Balinese style

ibu	mother, term of polite address to lady
ikat (endek)	cloth in which the threads are pattern-dyed before weaving
jalan	street, road (jalan jalan = walk, go)
jukung	outrigger canoe
kaja	in the direction of the mountains
klod (kelod)	in the direction of the sea
kris (keris)	dagger, often in serpentine shape
lamak	decorative strips of palm leaf
losmen	small local hotel
lumbung	rice barn with curved roof
mandi	tank of water for bathing (by filling a dipper and pouring water over yourself)
nusa	island
pantai	beach
pasar	market
penjor	decorated bamboo pole in front of house or beside road
prahu	outrigger sailing or motorized boat
puri	palace
songket	fabric woven with gold and silver thread

Numbers

1	**satu**	7	**tujuh**
2	**dua**	8	**delapan**
3	**tiga**	9	**sembilan**
4	**empat**	10	**sepuluh**
5	**lima**	11	**sebelas**
6	**enam**	12	**duabelas**

20	**duapuluh**	200	**dua ratus**
21	**duapuluh satu**	1000	**seribu**
30	**tigapuluh**	2000	**dua ribu**
100	**seratus**		

LAUNDRY *(cucian)* and DRY-CLEANING

Many hotels have same-day or next-day laundry and dry-cleaning services, at a price. Smaller places may be hard on the clothes and lack the means of thorough drying in rainy weather. Many hotels provide a bamboo rack for hanging out your own washing to dry.

LOST PROPERTY *(barang-barang hilang)*

If loss or suspected theft occur in your hotel, check first at the reception desk. They may suggest that you report the incident to the police. This may be time-consuming but necessary for any insurance claim. For something lost elsewhere, try retracing your steps to the shops or restaurants you visited; the management may have found it.

M

MAPS *(peta)*

Hotel shops and bookshops in the resort areas have good road maps of Bali and Lombok, but to be sure of getting the best it may be worth going to a specialist map shop in your home country before you begin your holiday.

MEDIA

Newspapers *(surat kabar)* **and magazines** *(majalah)*. A number of Jakarta newspapers are published in English editions and reach Bali the same day. The major resort hotels have the Singapore-printed *Asian Wall Street Journal* and *International Herald Tribune*, and several Australian papers by the same evening or next morning. The free *Bali News* and *Bali Tourist Guide* are worth looking for (try airline offices). They contain a lot of useful information although their articles and recommendations inevitably favour their advertisers.

Have you any newspapers in English?	**Apakah anda mempunyai koran dalam bahasa Inggris?**

Radio (*radio*) **and TV** (*televisi*). Local channels rarely broadcast anything of interest to foreigners, but larger hotels have satellite TV, with U.S. and Australian news channels. Radio Australia, BBC World Service, and Voice of America are well-received on short wave.

MEDICAL CARE (See also WATER on page 127)

Well before leaving home, ask your travel agent if any **immunizations** (vaccinations) are required. Ask your doctor which are currently recommended (for instance, cholera, typhoid, hepatitis). Your polio and tetanus shots should be up to date.

The threat of **malaria** has receded and the World Health Organization no longer suggests taking anti-malaria tablets for visits to Bali and Lombok. But if you are going to Lombok's offshore islands (including the Gilis) and to islands farther east, precautions are strongly advised. Doctors and pharmacists in your own country will have up-to-date information. Take an effective insect repellent with you (gels are excellent) and apply to all bare skin and around ankles, even if they are covered, as soon as dusk falls. Mosquitoes may carry dengue fever, another good reason to avoid their bites.

Larger hotels have doctors on call and may have a clinic staffed by nurses. Denpasar's main **hospital** is Sanglah Public Hospital, Jalan Sanglah; tel. (0361) 227911.

Pharmacies (*apotik*). They are quite well-stocked and can make up prescriptions. Medical services must be paid for, and although charges are not high in comparison with many Western countries, you should be sure to take out travel insurance including medical expenses. Your travel agent or insurance company can advise.

If you arrive in Bali after flying through several time zones, take it easy the first couple of days. Doctors recommend that visitors eat lightly at first, drink plenty of (non-alcoholic) liquids, and get plenty of rest. Jetlag fatigue may only set in on the second day.

Many mild cases of traveller's diarrhoea are the result of a change in diet, too much sun, and time-zone changes. Drink plenty of liquids, rest, and eat lightly and the problem should go away in a day or two. Don't starve yourself: many people find a diet of plain rice, bananas, and tea to be effective. If you have continuing or more serious symptoms, including vomiting, get medical advice.

Be careful of the tropical sun. Fair-skinned visitors find it takes a mere few minutes to turn red, but sunscreen creams—not oils—with high protection factors (SPF 30 or more) are now recommended for *all* skins. The sun's rays are doubly lethal on the beach because of reflection from water and sand. Strong sunglasses are a good investment. Try to do your sunning in small doses the first few days and stay out of direct sunlight between 11am and 2pm.

Take a leaf out of the Indonesians' book: bathe or shower at least twice a day, and ideally whenever you come in from the street, beach, or a tour. Thongs make good indoor footwear, and in a small hotel or *losmen* wear them in the bathroom and shower. In the simplest sorts of accommodation, the bathroom may contain a waist-high tub of water (*mandi*) for bathing, and a dipper. Throw water over yourself, soap, and rinse. Don't get in the tub!

Dangerous animals. Although few snakes on Bali and Lombok are poisonous, avoid walking through vegetation at night. If someone is bitten, keep them as still as possible and transport them to hospital right away. Most of Bali's dogs look mangy, but they are very unlikely to bother you, except by barking all night.

Intestinal worms are common; some types enter through the soles of the feet, so don't go barefoot. Bilharzia is present in some areas: don't swim or even stand in fresh water unless it is fast-running or comes straight from a spring.

Food Hygiene. Staff in the hotels and restaurants catering to tourists should have been trained in food-handling. Even so, the fact that salad ingredients need to be soaked in a cleansing solution for 20 minutes, followed by a further 20 minutes in purified water, is an indication of the risks. Raw vegetables and salads should be avoided except in the better hotels. All fruit should be peeled. Meat and fish should be well-cooked (except for the stringently prepared sushi in good hotels and Japanese restaurants).

MONEY MATTERS

Currency. The Indonesian rupiah (Rp or IDR) comes in banknotes (bills) of Rp100, 500, 1,000, 5,000, 10,000, 20,000, and 50,000. There are 25, 50, 100, 500, and 1,000 rupiah coins.

Banks and Currency Exchange. Banks are open from 8 or 8:30am to noon or 2pm, Monday to Friday. Moneychangers keep longer hours. Denpasar airport's currency-exchange office is open round the clock, but charges commission. Some ATMs are beginning to appear in Denpasar and other major towns, and they will dispense rupiah and deduct the amount from your bank account. Hotels may exchange foreign currency, but not always at favourable rates. Money-changers usually give the best rates (compare more than one, if you have time). Some shops and restaurants will accept major foreign currencies at a fair rate. Always count the money you are given when changing.

Credit Cards. All but the least expensive hotels accept major credit cards and charge cards. So do some restaurants, stores, and car rental companies, but they may add 3-5% to prices to cover the commission they will have to pay. You may be asked for your passport as extra identification. Some banks and big money-changers will advance cash against a credit card, but they'll take a 4, 5, or even 8% commission.

Traveller's Cheques. Hotels, tour operators, shops, and restaurants will accept traveller's checks in major currencies (e.g., U.S. and Australian dollars, yen, Deutsche marks, and pounds sterling) and they can also be changed at banks and moneychangers.

I want to change some pounds/dollars.	**Saya akan menukarkan beberapa uang pound sterling/dollar.**
Do you accept traveller's cheques?	**Apakah anda menerima pembayaran dengan traveller cheque?**

Bali

PLANNING YOUR BUDGET

To give you an idea of what to expect in Bali, here's a list of some average prices. They must be regarded as approximate, however, as inflation gradually drives them up.

Airport transfer. Taxi to Kuta Rp8,000, to Sanur Rp15,000. From Mataram (Lombok) to Senggigi Rp15,000.

Babysitters. Rp4,000 per hour.

Bemos. Sanur-Denpasar Rp600; Denpasar-Ubud Rp1,800.

Bicycle and motorcycle rental. Bicycle Rp45,000 a day, motorcycle Rp20,000 a day.

Car rental. Jeep-type vehicles Rp55,000-70,000 per day plus Rp10,000 per day for insurance.

Petrol (gasoline, called *Premium*) Rp700 per litre; diesel ("Solar") Rp380 per litre.

Guides. Brief temple tour Rp3,000. Half-day Rp40,000.

Hotels (double room with bath). Lower-price category Rp40,000, medium priced Rp100,000, higher priced Rp200,000, luxury Rp400,000 and up.

Losmen/homestay room with own *mandi* Rp10,000-20,000 including simple breakfast.

Meals and drinks. In resort hotels: breakfast Rp17,000; lunch or dinner Rp25,000; coffee Rp2,000, beer Rp4,000, wine (bottle) Rp50,000 and up.

Restaurants in tourist areas: Breakfast Rp6,000; lunch/dinner Rp10,000.

Local eating places: Breakfast Rp1,500; lunch/dinner Rp4,000.

Litre bottle of water Rp1,000; bottle of soft drink Rp750.

Sightseeing. Day tours Rp40,000-100,000.

Snorkel equipment. Rp6,000-10,000 per day.

Taxis. Rp1,000 minimum. Always negotiate in advance.

O

OPENING HOURS (See also PUBLIC HOLIDAYS on page 124)
Most **shops** are open from 9am-9pm every day; some close on Sunday. **Businesses** may open from 8am-4pm or 9am-5pm, Monday to Friday. **Government offices** operate from 8am-3pm Monday to Thursday and from 8-11:30am Friday.

Museums open from around 8am-2pm most days, but from 8-11am on Fridays and may close early on Saturdays and Sundays. The Le Mayeur Museum in Sanur is closed on Sundays and Mondays.

P

PHOTOGRAPHY *(fotografi)* **and VIDEO** *(video)*
The best times are early morning when the air is clearer, and late afternoon when the light is at its golden best. Your main enemy is the heat: avoid leaving cameras in direct sun or closed vehicles. Another problem: lenses mist over when you leave cold air-conditioning and come out into the humid air. Allow time for them to clear naturally.

Some temples and other sites charge a small fee for photography and in some places flash is banned. Local people resent being used as picture fodder. If you ask permission, in words or sign language, most of them will say no.

Most popular film makes and sizes are available. Colour print films can be quickly processed locally but transparency film is best kept until you get home. Airport X-ray machines are safe for all but ultra-fast film.

For tips on taking holiday snaps, try the Berlitz-Nikon *Guide to Travel Photography* (available in the U.K. only).

May I take a picture?   **Bolehkah saya memotret?**

Video. The standard types of tape are widely available. If you are buying pre-recorded tapes, make sure they are compatible with the system in your home country.

POLICE (*polisi*)
Regular police wear dark brown uniforms with a badge showing their name and number. Traffic police have a white or green cap and drive both marked and unmarked vehicles.

Personnel are normally polite and friendly, but matters move slowly and bureaucratically in police offices.

PUBLIC HOLIDAYS (*hari raya*)
The following are national holidays observed in Indonesia. Public offices and banks close, but shops, especially in tourist areas, will usually be open. In addition to the few holidays listed below, many Islamic, Buddhist, Hindu, and some Christian holidays are observed; many of these are governed by the lunar calendar and move from year to year. Bali's Chinese community also celebrates several of its own holidays.

1 January	**New Year's Day**
17 August	**Independence Day**
25 December	**Christmas Day**

R

RELIGION (*agama*)
Freedom of worship is written into the constitution. Most Indonesians are Muslim, with small minorities of Buddhists, Taoists, and Christians. Balinese people are almost all followers of their special form of Hinduism. Most people on Lombok are Muslim, with a substantial Bali-Hindu minority.

There are Roman Catholic churches in Denpasar and Tuban, and mass is also held at the Grand Bali Beach Hotel, Sanur, and Bali Sol Hotel, Nusa Dua. Protestant churches are in Denpasar, Tuban, and Legian. Numerous mosques include one in the Grand Bali Beach Hotel. Ask at the front desk of your hotel for times and exact locations of places of worship.

T

TIME DIFFERENCES
Bali and Lombok are on GMT (UTC) + 7. The chart shows the time in various cities in winter.

New York	London	Jo'burg	**Bali**	Sydney	Auckland
midnight	5am	7am	**noon**	3pm	5pm

TIPPING
A service charge of 10% is added to most hotel and some restaurant bills, but tipping is not expected in small local eating places. It's appropriate to give a small tip to porters for their services. The chart below gives some suggestions as to how much to leave.

Taxi-drivers	**Rp300-600**
Personal drivers and guides	**10%**
Porters	**Rp500 per bag**

TOILETS/RESTROOMS *(kamar kecil)*
All hotels intended for Western visitors have Western-style facilities. Elsewhere they are likely to be simpler, and in rural areas rudimentary or nonexistent. Carry your own paper when travelling round the islands. Where there are no flush toilets, use the dipper and tub of water provided for flushing. Ask for the WC ("way say") or *kamar kecil*.

TOURIST INFORMATION OFFICES *(kantor turis)*
Local offices have little printed material but may be able to tell you about the venues, dates, and times of events and ceremonies.
Denpasar: Kanwil Depparpostel X Bali & NTB, Komplex Niti Mandala, Jalan Raya Puputan, Renon; tel. (0361) 225649.
Badung Tourist Promotion Board, Jalan Bakung Sari 1, Renon; tel. (0361) 756176.
Mataram, Lombok: Kanwil Depparpostel NTB, Jalan Indrakila 2A; tel. (0370) 22327.

Bali

Indonesian tourist promotion offices in other countries:

Australia: Level 10, 5 Elizabeth Street, Sydney 2000; tel. (02) 233-3630; fax (02) 233-3629.

UK: 3 Hanover Street, London; tel. (0171) 493-0030; fax (0171) 493-1747.

USA: 3457 Wilshire Blvd, Los Angeles CA90010; tel. (213) 387-2078; fax (213) 380-4876.

TRANSPORT

Buses (*bis*). They are cheap but generally overcrowded. It is more comfortable to take a *bemo*. Budget travellers use the long-distance buses that connect with inter-island ferries to Java and Lombok.

Taxis (*taksi*). There are supposed to be fixed official rates for all journeys but most drivers will charge as much as they can get away with. Try to find out the approved rate, and always agree upon the fare in advance unless there is a meter. Even if taxis have meters, drivers try to avoid using them or to persuade you that they have the right to charge much more. Insist that meters are switched on; you will never be able to negotiate anything lower than the meter rate.

Bemos. Minivans follow a fixed route, picking up and setting down passengers, and some are painted according to their usual destination—try to get to know the colours. Prices are fixed but you will be overcharged unless you know the right fare. Watch what others pay.

Dokars. Tiny ponies pull two-wheeled carts, often laden with passengers or sacks of rice. Decide fares before boarding. (The word *dokar* comes from the English "dog-cart," a pony-and-trap once used to carry dogs.) In Lombok, a *cidomo* is similar, but with car tyres.

Ferries (*ferry*). Car and passenger ferry services connect Gilimanuk in west Bali with Java; Padangbai in east Bali with Lembar, Lombok; and Labuan Lombok in east Lombok to the island of Sumbawa. A faster passenger ferry runs from Benoa Port near Denpasar to Lembar. In addition, small boats sail to the inhabited offshore islands on demand, if anyone is prepared to pay.

Inter-island Flights. Various local airlines operate many times a day from Denpasar to Mataram, Lombok—it's virtually a shuttle service. Both islands are also connected frequently to their neighbours and thus to all main centres in Indonesia.

TRAVELLERS WITH DISABILITIES

Only the most modern hotels cater to the needs of travellers with disabilities. The cottage design adopted by many means they are spread out, sometimes on a hilly site. Temples include many steps and pavements (sidewalks) are littered with hazards and obstacles.

Airlines should always be notified in advance when a disabled person is to travel.

TRAVELLING TO BALI and LOMBOK

By Air. Many international airlines fly to Denpasar direct. Competitive prices are widely advertised. Book early if travelling at peak season (July-September and around Christmas).

There are no international flights to Lombok; you generally have to change planes at Denpasar.

Package Holidays and Tours. The range of holidays offered is vast. Flights, hotel, and breakfast are normally included. Excursions may be extra. Always study the small print.

W

WATER *(air)*

Although tap water should be regarded as unsafe, the best hotels do purify their own. The carafe water in some hotels should have been purified; otherwise keep to bottled water and bottled drinks (make sure the seal is unbroken). To sterilize water, boil it for 20 minutes or add a purifying tablet, following the instructions. Ice production is subject to government control and inspection, so ice should be safe.

Is this drinking water?   **Apakah air ini boleh diminum?**

Bali

WEIGHTS and MEASURES (For distance and fluid measures see
DRIVING on page 112)
Indonesia uses the metric system.

Length

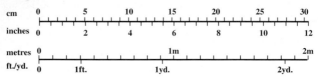

Weight

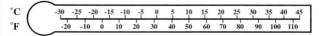

Temperature

| °C | -30 -25 -20 -15 -10 -5 0 5 10 15 20 25 30 35 40 45 |
| °F | -20 -10 0 10 20 30 40 50 60 70 80 90 100 110 |

WOMEN TRAVELLERS

Women travelling alone in Bali can anticipate constant approaches
on the beaches, in the bars, or even in the street from would-be es-
corts. Some are simply friendly, some are trying their luck, and others are thieves after money.

Lombok, with its Islamic tradition, is less accustomed to independent women. Expect to be stared at.

YOUTH HOSTELS

There is one IHYA-registered hostel in Bali: Bali International Youth
Hostel, Jalan Mertasari 19, Banjar Suwung Kangin, Sidakarya; tel.
(0361) 263912. A few simple homestays call themselves **hostels** and
some offer dormitory-style rooms with up to four beds.

A SELECTION
OF HOTELS
AND RESTAURANTS

Recommended Hotels

The hotels below are listed by geographical area and then alphabetically. The rates given are for a double room with private bathroom or shower, not including breakfast. Service and tax, totalling 21%, are additional. Room rates can be considerably lower as part of an inclusive package, and low-season discounts may be available. The busiest times are from July to September and from Christmas to late January: if you plan to visit then, make reservations well in advance. Except in the mountains where it is unnecessary, rooms have air-conditioning unless otherwise stated. Hotels in the larger towns are used mainly by local business travellers and probably won't appeal to holiday visitors.

You can also find simpler sorts of budget accommodation (see page 105), costing a fraction of the lowest price quoted here.

✪✪✪✪✪	over $200
✪✪✪✪	$120-200
✪✪✪	$60-120
✪✪	$30-60
✪	up to $30

SOUTHERN BALI

DENPASAR

Natour Bali ✪✪✪ *Jalan Veteran; Tel. (0361) 225681; Fax (0361) 235347.* 80 rooms. Central, near Puputan Square, with a garden and swimming pool. Built in the colonial era, once it was the only hotel in Bali. A more modern annexe has been added across the street.

JIMBARAN BEACH

Bali Inter-Continental Resort ✪✪✪✪ *Jalan Uluwatu 45,*

Jimbaran; Tel. (0361) 701888; Fax (0361) 701777. 425 rooms. An elaborate and luxurious resort resembling a Balinese palace, with remarkable water gardens. Facilities include tennis and squash courts, health club, swimming pools, and sailing club. Faces a vast curving beach of golden sand with fairly sheltered water. Restaurants include the notable oriental *Singaraja*.

Four Seasons Resort Bali ✪✪✪✪✪ *Jimbaran; Tel. (0361) 701010; Fax (0361) 701020.* 147 spacious villas, each with own walled garden, plunge pool, outdoor shower, and large indoor bath. The resort is set on a hillside overlooking Jimbaran Bay, and a short walk leads to a big sandy beach and watersports centre.

KUTA, LEGIAN, AND TUBAN BEACH

Bali Anggrek Inn ✪✪ *Jalan Pantai Kuta, Kuta; Tel. (0361) 751265; Fax (0361) 751766.* 151 rooms. A bright, modern hotel close to the centre of Kuta, set in gardens next to the main surfing beach. The swimming pool area is elevated, providing seclusion and beach views.

Bali Dynasty Resort ✪✪✪ *Julan Kartika Plaza, Tuban Beach 80361; Tel. (0361) 752403; Fax (0361) 752402.* 267 rooms. Managed by Shangri-La International and set in a quiet garden, not far from the broad sandy beach, with a swimming pool and tennis court. Noted for family atmosphere, dinner buffets, its disco and karaoke bar.

Bali Mandira Hotel ✪✪ *Jalan Padma, Legian; Tel. (0361) 751381; Fax (0361) 752377.* 120 rooms, mostly in modern, well-equipped cottages. The compound faces the broad Legian beach with surfing and swimming areas. Sports facilities include tennis and squash courts and large swimming pool in a quiet garden.

Bali Padma ✪✪✪ *Jalan Padma 1, Kuta; Tel. (0361) 752111; Fax (0361) 752140.* 400 rooms. In spacious grounds next to the beach, this is one of the newer and most luxurious resorts in central Legian, with tennis and squash courts and a large swimming pool. The Japanese restaurant has gained a reputation for authentic cuisine.

Bali

Bintang Bali ✪✪✪ *Jalan Kartika Plaza, Tuban Beach 80361; Tel. (0361) 753292; Fax (0361) 753288.* 401 rooms. A big resort hotel at the quieter southern end of this large stretch of sandy beach, popular with families and young Japanese. The swimming pool with waterfalls surrounds a stage used for dance performances. Facilities include tennis courts, a health club and sauna, water sports, a disco, and karaoke bar.

Oberoi Bali ✪✪✪✪✪ *Jalan Kayu Aya, Legian; Tel. (0361) 730361; Fax (0361) 730791.* 75 spacious and luxuriously equipped cottages and villas, amid beautiful gardens, north of Legian, next to a huge, white, and often deserted sandy beach. The Oberoi is highly rated for its standards of service and cuisine. There are frequent dance performances staged in an outdoor theatre.

Pertamina Cottages ✪✪✪✪ *Tuban Beach 80361; Tel. (0361) 751161; Fax (0361) 752030.* 206 rooms in attractive villas, built for the national oil company and expanded into an impressive resort. At the southern end of the Kuta-Tuban sandy beach, near the airport, with mature gardens, two swimming pools, and tennis courts.

Poppies Cottages ✪✪-✪✪✪ *off Poppies Gang, Kuta; Tel. (0361) 751059; Fax (0361) 752364.* 20 rooms in traditional brick cottages which have been upgraded to near-luxury standard over the years. Set in a small but well-designed garden compound with a swimming pool, across the way from Poppies restaurant in the middle of Kuta and quite near the beach. (Old Poppies Cottages in Legian offers slightly less luxurious rooms and no pool.)

NUSA DUA

Amanusa ✪✪✪✪✪ *Nusa Dua; Tel. (0361) 772333; Fax (0361) 772335.* 35 private villas, luxuriously appointed and with their own gardens, set on its own hilltop next to a golf course overlooking the Nusa Dua resort area. Facilities include a tennis court, large swimming pool, shuttle service to its own beach club, and water sports. The restaurant specialises in excellent Thai dishes.

Bali Hilton International ✪✪✪✪ *Nusa Dua Beach; Tel. (0361) 771102; Fax (0361) 771616.* 537 rooms. A palatial resort in the Nusa Dua enclave with spacious grounds and water gardens, adjoining a vast white-sand beach. Public areas are elaborate open-sided pavilions. Facilities include swimming pools, covered tennis courts, squash courts, a theatre, and a disco.

Puri Tanjung ✪✪ *Jalan Pratama 62, Nusa Dua; Tel. (0361) 772121; Fax (03621) 772424.* 64 rooms, in separate cottages and a garden wing. A modern hotel, popular with the European tour groups, north of the main Nusa Dua resort area. The large swimming pool is set in lush tropical gardens next to a white-sand beach.

Sheraton Nusa Indah ✪✪✪ *Nusa Dua Beach; Tel. (0361) 771906; Fax (0361) 771908.* 369 rooms. This is a spectacular resort hotel combined with a convention centre, facing the dazzling white-sand beach. Tennis courts, swimming pools, and water sports, restaurants, and other facilities at the hotel are augmented by those at the next-door **Sheraton Lagoon** (✪✪✪✪), where the swimming pool is indeed a lagoon. Two golf courses are close at hand.

SANUR

Bali Hyatt ✪✪✪✪ *Jalan Danau Tamblingan 89; Tel. (0361) 281234; Fax (0361) 287693.* 387 rooms. Long-established but completely renovated, this hotel features traditional Balinese architecture and decor. Set in spacious gardens next to a wide sand beach and sheltered water inside the Sanur reef, with tennis courts, two swimming pools, and a watersports centre.

Bali Sanur Bungalows ✪✪ *Jalan Hang Tuah, Samur; Tel. (0361) 288421; Fax (0361) 288426.* 177 rooms, simply decorated and furnished, in bungalows grouped into small "villages" with their own swimming pools. They are close to many shops and restaurants, and one block from the wide, sandy Sanur beach where a variety of watersports is offered.

Grand Bali Beach ✪✪✪✪ *Jalan Hangtuah; Tel. (0361) 288511; Fax (0361) 287917.* 600 rooms. On the beach facing the sheltered waters of Sanur reef. The low-rise garden wings and separate cottages are all set in an extensive park. Facilities include four swimming pools, tennis courts, watersports, a health club, indoor bowling, and a 9-hole golf course.

Sanur Beach ✪✪✪✪ *Semawang Samur, Denpasar; Tel. (0361) 288011; Fax (0361) 287566.* 425 rooms. This big resort hotel faces the southern end of Sanur Beach. Guest rooms are in several interconnecting wings facing the pools or garden courtyards. Facilities include tennis courts, badminton, three swimming pools and watersports, bicycle tours, and cultural performances. There are Thai, seafood, and other restaurants and a variety of shops.

Tandjung Sari ✪✪✪✪ *Sanur Beach; Tel. (0361) 288441; Fax (0361) 287930.* 28 separate bungalows built in local styles, using traditional materials and techniques. In some of them the bedroom is on the upper storey. A luxuriously equipped retreat, set in lovely tropical gardens with a swimming pool, next to the wide sandy beach. The restaurant rates as one of the best in the area.

UBUD AND VICINITY

Amandari ✪✪✪✪✪ *Kedewatan; Tel. (0361) 975333; Fax (0361) 975335.* 29 rooms, in separate traditional houses, some with upper-storey bedrooms and private pools. The resort is designed as a walled village in Balinese style with beautiful stonework, wonderful views over the Ayung gorge, and a large swimming pool. It makes a good centre for walking, biking, or rafting on the Ayung river.

Cahaya Dewata Hotel & Villas ✪✪-✪✪✪ *Kedewatan; Tel. (0361) 975495; Fax (0361) 974349.* 42 rooms, mostly in bungalows. Sited on the edge of the Ayung river valley, the hotel offers spectacular views from many of the rooms, the swimming pool area, and restaurant. It's only a short journey but a world away from the busy centre of Ubud.

Puri Padi ✪✪✪ *Jalan Hanoman, Padang Tegal; Tel. (0361) 975075; Fax (0361) 975740.* 28 rooms in newly-built Balinese-style bungalows, with peaceful views over rice paddies and a river valley. Near the Ubud-Pengesokan road, convenient for visiting dance performances, the town centres, and art galleries. There's a swimming pool and a quiet garden.

Tjampuhan ✪✪-✪✪✪ *Campuhan; Tel. (0361) 975368; Fax (0361) 975137.* 55 rooms in attractive thatched cottages. The hotel was the site of the house built by artist Walter Spies in the 1930s, in a lush garden setting on slopes above the Campuhan river valley. Although close to the centre of Ubud, it's reasonably quiet. There are two swimming pools and tennis and badminton courts. Nightly dance performances are staged nearby.

Ulun Ubud Cottages ✪✪ *Sanggingan, off Ubud-Campuhan road; Tel. (0361) 975024; Fax (0361) 975524.* 27 quite spacious, well-equipped rooms in traditional cottages. They are beautifully positioned on a steep hillside looking down into the valley of the Campuhan river. Many fine carvings decorate the gardens and the landscaped swimming pool area. A convenient base for walking or cycling.

EASTERN BALI

Kusamajaya Beach Inn ✪ *Jemelak, Amlapura; Tel. (0363) 21250; no Fax.* 8 rooms, not air-conditioned, in attractive small bungalows, located on the almost deserted northeast coast 3 km (2 miles) east of Amed, next to a narrow sandy beach with fishing boats. There is a simple restaurant. Very good snorkelling and diving are the two main attractions of the area.

Tirta Ayu ✪ *Tirta Gangga, Amlapura; Tel. (0363) 21697; no Fax.* 4 rooms, plainly furnished, in small cottages in a compound inside the Water Palace area, set in the hills above Amlapura. There's a simple restaurant. The main attractions here are the cool air and the magnificent views over beautiful, lush rice terraces. Hotel guests can go swimming in the unique spring-fed pools of the water garden.

CANDI DASA/ BALINA BEACH

Royale Bali Beach Club ✪✪ *Balina Beach, Manggis; Tel. (0363) 41021; Fax via (0363) 41022.* 20 plain rooms, all with balconies or patios, face a small garden courtyard and a swimming pool. Situated 3 km (2 miles) west of Candi Dasa, this hotel adjoins the beach of dark-sand and stones.

Rama Ocean View Bungalows ✪✪✪ *Candi Dasa Beach; Tel. via (0361) 233974; Fax (0361) 233975.* 42 modern, well-equipped rooms in traditionally designed cottages, set in lovely gardens, next to the dark-sand beach (narrow at high tide). Plenty of activities are available, with tennis courts, a sauna, a large swimming pool; watersports including snorkelling and diving around offshore islets.

PADANGBAI

Rai Beach Inn ✪ *Jalan Silayukti ; no Tel.* This inn has 21 rooms in simple but pleasant cottages, not air-conditioned. Each has a saltwater shower and freshwater *mandi*. Facing the sheltered beach and fishing village, and close to the little port (for the ferry to Lombok). Its dining room is one of the best places to eat in Padangbai.

NORTHERN BALI

LOVINA

Aditya Bungalows ✪✪ *Lovina Beach; Tel. (0362) 41059; Fax (0362) 41342.* 80 rooms in plain two-storey buildings, each with a balcony or patio, set in gardens next to a long stretch of dark-sand beach. Popular with European tour groups. There's a large restaurant, elevated swimming pool, and watersports, including fishing, dolphin watching, windsurfing, and snorkelling. Diving expeditions can be arranged.

Bali Lovina Beach Cottages ✪✪ *Lovina Beach; Tel. (0362) 412664; Fax (0362) 41478.* 34 rooms. Comfortable traditional-style cottages face compact gardens adjoining a long stretch of black-sand beach. There's a swimming pool, and watersports include wind-surfing and excellent snorkelling on the nearby reef.

Palma Beach ✪✪✪ *Lovina Beach; Tel. (0362) 41775; Fax (0362) 41659.* 50 rooms, mostly in separate cottages or villas, are newly built but in attractive traditional styles, set round spacious gardens with a swimming pool and tennis courts.

MOUNTAINS

Amertha's Homestay ✪ *Toyo Bungkah, Kintamani; no Tel.* 8 rooms, plainly furnished, some in separate bungalows, in a village on the floor of the *caldera* of Mount Batur, next to the crater lake. The terrace of the simple restaurant has a spectacular view. You can bathe in a small pool fed by hot springs. This makes a good base for hikes and climbing Batur.

Bali Handara Kosaido Country Club ✪✪✪ *Pancasari, Bedugul; Tel. (0362) 22646; Fax (0362) 23048.* 77 rooms in bungalows and the main building are modern and well-equipped. The club is mainly used by golfers who come to play the championship course. There are also tennis courts, a health club, and sauna.

Pancasari Inn ✪✪ *Pancasari, Bedugul; Tel. and Fax (0362) 21148.* 11 rooms in separate modern cottages, in a cool mountain village set on the slopes of Gunung Batur, close to the crater lakes and to the Bali Handara Country Club golf course. This is also great countryside for walking or cycling. The inn has its own tennis court.

Puri Lumbung ✪✪ *Munduk; Tel. (0362) 92514; Fax via (0361) 71532.* 5 rooms in traditional ricebarn-style cottages, built on a hillside in a village west of Lake Tamblingan. Superb views over rice terraces. This is an excellent area for walking, cycling, and canoeing. It is also within easy reach of northcoast beaches.

WEST BALI

Medewi Beach Cottages ✪✪ *Pekutatan, Jembrana; Tel. (0365) 40029; Fax (0365) 41555.* 36 rooms in nicely designed new cottages, in pretty gardens with a good-sized swimming pool. It stands close to a small sandy beach, but the main attraction is the surfing. About 70 km (43 miles) west of Denpasar.

LOMBOK

Lombok Intan Laguna ✪✪✪ *Jalan Senggigi; Tel. (0364) 93090; Fax (0364) 93185.* 209 rooms facing well-shaded gardens adjoining the sandy beach. There is a large landscaped swimming pool, a tennis court, and a watersports centre. Dance performances and outdoor barbecues and buffets are put on in the evenings.

Pacific Beach Cottages ✪✪ *Kerandangan, Senggigi; Tel. and Fax (0364) 93027.* 26 rooms, in separate cottages, are compact but well-equipped, with terraces facing the sea, next to a narrow dark-sand beach at the northern end of the Senggigi resort area. There is quite good snorkelling, and diving expeditions can be arranged.

Senggigi Beach ✪✪✪ *Jalan Senggigi; Tel. (0364) 93339; Fax (0364) 93185.* 150 rooms. Dramatically sited on a headland, the rooms are well equipped and comfortable, some in bungalows, others in two-storey buildings. A full range of watersports is offered: diving trips can be arranged. Nightly outdoor dining events and frequent cultural shows are staged.

Sheraton Senggigi Beach ✪✪✪✪ *Mataram; Tel. (0364) 93333; Fax (0364) 93140.* 156 rooms, attractively furnished, in three-storey buildings set in beautifully tended, shaded gardens next to a sandy beach. Among the facilities here are tennis courts, an elaborately designed swimming pool, watersports centre offering snorkelling and sailing, a health club, and a disco. Fishing and diving trips can be arranged. Frequent outdoor dining events and cultural performances are staged.

Recommended Restaurants

Most restaurants are found in or near resort areas. They are aimed at visitors and charge considerably more than places meant for local people. Many of the best restaurants are in hotels (see our Recommended Hotels list starting on p130), where prices may be higher again, although still reasonable by international standards. At one time, the vast majority of eating places had remarkably similar menus, all featuring the same staple dishes based on either rice or noodles. Then the choice widened to include Mexican, Thai, Japanese, Italian, Indian, and other national styles. These rarely taste quite authentic — the spices and oils are different — but they can still be very enjoyable in the local version.

The price indication given below is for a starter, main course, and dessert, per person. A charge is often added for service and tax. This is not consistent but 10% is typical.

✪✪✪	over $10
✪✪	$6-10
✪	up to $6

SOUTHERN BALI

DENPASAR

Atoom Baru ✪✪ *Jalan Gajah Mada 106; Tel. (0361) 222733.* This is a big Chinese-Indonesian restaurant in a central location between Puputan Square and the market area. Atoom Baru offers a long menu including seafood and spicy dishes from Sumatra. It is favoured by local business people at lunchtime, and is also a popular venue for family parties.

Bali

Simpang Enam ✪ *Jalan Teuku Umar 65; Tel. (0361) 226646.* In a street lined with a variety of cheap eating places, this simple local dining room serves the basic rice and noodles found almost everywhere, but also features some Balinese specialities: chicken lawar, minced seafood satays, and roast duck with spices.

Taman Bali ✪ *Jalan Cokroaminoto 288, (Raya Ubung, km 6); Tel. (0361) 434617.* Indonesian, Chinese, and seafood dishes served here include all the standard items: nasi goreng, ayam goreng, babi guling (spit-roast pork), as well as more ambitious Chinese menus. This is a popular place with local families.

JIMBARAN

Puncak Pesona ✪✪ *Jalan Raya Uluwatu; Tel. (0361) 229055.* With an attractive terrace setting on a hill overlooking the arc of Jimbaran Bay, this is a modern restaurant serving Chinese, Indonesian, and some fairly authentic Japanese food.

KUTA, LEGIAN, AND TUBAN BEACH

Bali Indah ✪✪ *Jalan Buni Sari 17, Kuta; Tel. (0361) 751937.* An open-fronted dining room right in the middle of the busiest section of Kuta serves standard Indonesian and Chinese dishes, plus good quality fresh seafood. (There is another branch in the slightly quieter Jalan Melasti, Legian.)

Bali Seafood ✪✪ *Jalan Kartika Plaza, Tuban; Tel. (0361) 753902.* In a big bright hall, a restaurant that mostly operates by the "supermarket" system: you pick out your own fish, giant prawns, etc., and the rest of the ingredients of your dinner and hand them over to be cooked. Items are charged by weight, and a cooking fee is added.

Double Six ✪✪ *Jalan Double Six, Seminyak, Legian; Tel. (0361) 753366.* This large, open-air beachside nightspot serves reliable Italian dishes and good grilled seafood. It becomes one of Bali's liveliest discos later in the evening, staying open until dawn.

Gado Gado ✪✪ *Jalan Dhyana Pura, Seminyak, Legian; Tel. (0361) 752255.* Gado Gado is an attractive terrace restaurant with a beach and sunset view, serving good Thai and other Asian dishes. The adjoining night club and disco gets going around midnight and runs until dawn.

Harbour Pizzeria ✪✪ *Jalan Melasti (beach end), Legian; Tel. (0361) 751770.* With a view of one of the liveliest parts of the beach, this open-air terrace restaurant is much more than a popular kind of Western pizzeria serving pizza and pasta. There are theme nights and barbecues, satays, seafood, and elaborate desserts, too.

Kuta Seafood and Music House ✪✪✪ *Jalan Kartika Plaza, Tuban; Tel. (0361) 755807.* Despite the name, this big seafood "palace" is south of Kuta near the Tuban Beach hotels. You can select your own whole fish or live lobster, at a price (measured according to weight). There's entertainment by local groups playing mostly Western music.

LG Club ✪✪ *Jalan Legian, off Jalan Double Six, Kuta; Tel. (0361) 751131.* A big and bright restaurant, specializing in fresh fish and also offering fairly authentic Japanese and Korean dishes served as a buffet. Balinese dance and music performances are staged. There is a separate karaoke bar.

Poppies ✪✪✪ *Poppies Gang, Kuta; Tel. (0361) 75109.* Established over 20 years ago and still the fashionable favourite. In an elegant garden setting off an alleyway right in the middle of Kuta, it serves reliable Western and Indonesian dishes and good fresh seafood.

Rum Jungle Road International ✪✪ *Jalan Pura Bagus Taruna, Legian; Tel. (0361) 751992.* The choice of many

Australians and New Zealanders looking for their kind of cooking. Meats are imported from New Zealand, and steaks and seafood are specialities, with Indonesian dishes also on the menu. Accommodation is available, too, with a swimming pool.

TJ's Mexican ✪✪ *Poppies Gang, Kuta; Tel. (0361) 751093.* In an attractive garden setting, this place has been long celebrated as the best Mexican food west of the Pacific.

NUSA DUA/BENOA

Matsuri ✪✪✪ *Galleria Nusa Dua, Block B14; Tel. (0361) 772267.* One of 9 eating places in Nusa Dua's shopping centre, this bright Japanese restaurant has a sushi bar and an authentic menu. Free transport from Nusa Dua hotels.

Ulam ✪✪ *Jalan P. Mengiat, Peminge 14, Bualu; Tel. (0361) 771590.* This indoor and outdoor restaurant near to the Nusa Dua resort hotels is noted for Balinese, Indonesian, and especially seafood dishes, such as grilled fish with sambal matah.

SANUR

Batu Jimbar ✪ *Jalan D. Tamblingan; Tel. (0361) 287374.* Menu of mainly vegetarian dishes and sandwiches are served in a café combined with a cakeshop and bookshop. It is a popular rendezvous for tea and snacks.

Kul Kul ✪ *Jalan D. Tamblingan 166; Tel. (0361) 288038.* One of many eating places along the road near the Sanur hotels, it has an attractive open-air garden setting. The typical Indonesian menu of rice and noodles with chicken or seafood offers some basic Western dishes as well.

Lenny's ✪✪ *Jalan Pantai; Tel. (0361) 287975.* A long-established restaurant in a new location specializes in fish and shellfish, some still swimming or crawling as they wait to be chosen by customers. There is a separate karaoke bar. Free transport can be arranged from the hotels in Sanur. (Another branch of Lenny's can be found in Kuta.)

Telaga Naga ✪✪✪ *Jalan D. Tamblingan; Tel. (0361) 288271.* Open-air pavilion beautifully sited on a high terrace over gardens and ponds. Authentic Chinese regional dishes are excellent.

UBUD AND VICINITY

Café Wayan ✪ *Jalan Monkey Forest (South end); no Tel.* A family-operated, bright, and cheerful café serving good Indonesian dishes, plus pizzas, reliable salads, and other international standards. It has a pleasant, quiet open-air garden.

Griya ✪✪ *Jalan Raya, Ubud; Tel. (0361) 975428.* A friendly restaurant centrally located in the busy town, set in the open air above street level. It specializes in grills: fish, steaks, and tasty barbecued chicken.

Lilies Garden ✪ *Jalan Monkey Forest, Ubud; Tel. (0361) 975359.* A modern and friendly café serving standard Chinese and Indonesian food and also Western snacks, salads, and desserts.

Murni's ✪✪✪ *Campuhan, Ubud; Tel. (0361) 975233.* Still sometimes known as Murni's Warung, it is the long-established and fashionable place to eat in Ubud. Murni's serves local and Western dishes, on a terrace overlooking the Campuhan river valley. Accommodation is available.

EASTERN BALI

BALINA/CANDI DASA

TJ's Café ✪✪ *Candi Dasa; Tel. (0363) 41450.* An attractive two-level terrace restaurant above the main road in the middle of Candi Dasa. Operated by the same people as TJ's in Kuta, it serves

Mexican dishes and also a range of seafood, vegetarian, and wholefood, burgers, and chips.

Ubud ✪ *Buitan, Manggis; no Tel.* A tiny, family-run restaurant on an open-air terrace serving standard Indonesian and Chinese dishes, and excellent fresh fish, generally thick steaks of barracuda, tuna, or shark. Tables not taken by diners are often used by the children doing their homework.

Wiratha ✪ *Candi Dasa; Tel. (0363) 41973.* Close to the beach in central Candi Dasa, a big, brash café, bar, and restaurant serving a whole range of multinational dishes: Chinese, Indonesian, and Italian food, fresh fish, and fast food.

NORTHERN BALI

LOVINA/SINGARAJA

Segar II ✪ *Jalan Jenderal A. Yani, Singaraja; Tel. (0362) 21832.* An informal local dining room set back from a wide, busy street, serving a simple menu of Chinese, Indonesian, and fish dishes, this place is known for its good food.

MOUNTAINS

Rama ✪✪ *Penelokan, Kintamani; Tel. (0362) 23465.* One of many big restaurants catering to the lunchtime rush of tour buses, but independent travellers are naturally welcome. This one stands out for the range and quality of dishes, Chinese, Indonesian, Indian, and Western, on its buffets. Closed in the evenings.

WEST BALI

Taman Senggulan ✪ *Jalan Jenderal Subroto 1, Tabanan; Tel. (0361) 811005.* On the eastern exit from the town, this big glass dining hall is convenient if you have been on an expedition to the west of Bali. A local gathering place for parties and functions, it serves a long menu of Chinese and seafood dishes.